HEINEMANN SCHOOL MANAGEMENT

LAUNCESTON ROAD   thelearninginstitute
CALLINGTON
CORNWALL PL17 7DR

Observing Teachers at Work

by
Grace Marriott

To the hundreds of good teachers in schools all over England whose lessons I have been privileged to watch over the past ten years.

Heinemann Educational Publishers
Halley Court, Jordan Hill, Oxford OX2 8EJ
a division of Reed Educational & Professional Publishing Ltd

OXFORD   MELBOURNE   AUCKLAND
JOHANNESBURG   BLANTYRE   GABORONE
IBADAN   PORTSMOUTH (NH) USA   CHICAGO

Heinemann is a registered trademark of Reed Educational & Professional Publishing Ltd

First published in 2001

05 04 03 02 01
10 9 8 7 6 5 4 3 2 1

British Library Cataloguing in Publication Data
A catalogue record for this book is available from the British Library

ISBN   0 435 800620

Typeset by Wyvern 21 Ltd., Bristol
Printed and bound in Great Britain by Biddles Ltd., Guildford

Acknowledgements
The author would like to thank the following:
Maeve Willis, Susan Malyon and Peter Watson for reading and commenting on the text; Michael Marland, Sue Walton, Robert Bircher and Stephani Havard for their guidance and attention to detail; Addington High School, Croydon, for permission to use the observation forms developed for use with newly qualified teachers and other staff; Rosebery School, Epsom, for permission to use the observation form developed as part of the school's internal review procedures.
The publishers have made every effort to contact copyright holders. However, if any material has been incorrectly acknowledged, the publishers would be pleased to correct this at the earliest opportunity.

Tel: 01865 888058 www.heinemann.co.uk

Contents

Preface
by Michael Marland, Series Editor

The core of supportive personal and professional leadership is knowing an individual's work in detail and recognising its special qualities. Thus, school management has observation of the teachers' work at its core, vital for the professional pride of the teachers, their career development, overall school planning and central government requirements. In past decades, however, there has been insufficient attention paid to the personal, professional, logistical and definitional problems of observing teachers. Indeed, in the first school in which I taught, one well-established figure declared firmly, 'No-one's been in my classroom for forty years – and they're not starting now!' Times have certainly changed, but the legacy of that attitude still lingers. It could be argued that of the range of managerial tasks in schools, despite central government pressure in the last decade of the twentieth century (or perhaps because of it!), the specific observation of the teachers' work has been one of the less carefully analysed aspects of education. The *Heinemann School Management Series* has often included the topic, starting with the first book in the Series in 1971: 'The Head of Department must know what goes on in the classes for which he (or she) is responsible.'

Observation of teachers' work has seriously suffered from its past reputation and the limited purpose it has sometimes been seen as having. This book in its depth, breadth and sensitive practicality takes observation beyond the 'problems of beginners' role to a whole-school management strength. In the early twenty-first century, the full range of observation is required not only because of the central government requirements for Newly Qualified Teachers (NQTs), for Threshold Assessment and for overall Performance Management, but also for the personal and professional pride and satisfaction of the individual teachers. Sadly, it is too often discussed as if 'observation' is linked only to finding faults and observing weaknesses. However, Grace Marriott makes clear that the observation not only helps professionals to work on any weaknesses, but it is deeply appreciated for the recognition of skill and success.

Although the author's overall approach is properly holistic, Grace Marriott helpfully focuses on the different occasions: whether the whole class or specific groups, whether the overall lesson or specific aspects. Further, she appreciates the differences deriving from the position of the observer, whether head of course department, pastoral middle management, or senior management. She also includes very practically observation by school governors, and highlights their valuable lay vision.

The observation needs to be whole-school planned in terms both of individuals and activities. It is obviously required for NQTs, but it is also appreciated by and helpful for the most experienced and senior. It is most often thought of for subject-course lessons, but also, Grace Marriott stresses, it is important for pastoral care. Too often discussions of teacher observation have related only to 'subject' lessons and the important pastoral dimension is not included. Grace Marriott importantly includes this, from the tutorial period to individual interviews of pupils and their parents – a difficult skill that has been insufficiently considered nationally and very rarely observed.

In the professional climate of recent years, the value to the *observed* has been over-emphasised at the expense of the contribution it also makes to the understanding of the *observer*, not only for her or his own knowledge, but for its contribution to curriculum planning, pastoral care, staffing, logistics and overall ethos. As the country's secondary schools determinedly work to come out of the over-domination of discrete 'subject' courses and develop appropriate inter-linking and mutual support of the different activities, well managed observation has a very key part to play in informing whole-school planning. For instance, observation is required to establish the contribution of a particular subject lesson, such as Science or History, to overall literacy, numeracy, citizenship, or personal and social development.

Grace Marriott brings extensive experience in secondary-school middle and senior management together with her substantial advisory and inspectoral role and her in-school training work to help all those with responsibility positions in schools and the Governors. She fully incorporates the requirements of the DfEE and the recommendations of the Teacher Training Agency. Further, the full text of the 'Key Findings' of the Hay McBer *Research into Teacher Effectiveness* is included as it relates to so many aspects of observing teachers. Her book enables a secondary school further to develop its observation policy and practice as an integral part of successful, positive, whole-school management, review and planning. She shows how this encourages staff pride and satisfaction. This is one of the first UK books devoted entirely to this key activity and skill. We see it as a very important addition to the twenty-first century's strengthened focus on school management and Grace Marriott's significant experience and focus on this work as a key part of the *School Management Series* overview.

# Why observe teachers at work?: the justification for regular and systematic observation

Observing teachers at work has long been part of the normal routine in many schools, mainly because staff realise that timely and effective observation and feedback are of immense value. They are helpful to the individuals in terms of developing their own professional expertise and giving them support and encouragement. In relation to school development, the more information a school has on the quality of teaching and learning, that is, on what actually happens in classrooms, the more effective the planning to raise and maintain standards is likely to be.

Statutory requirements and national expectations

Observation is not a new idea and for some aspects of teaching it has long been a requirement: for example beginning teachers and newly qualified teachers (NQTs) have always been observed. The introduction of the statutory teacher appraisal scheme made it a requirement at least once every two years for almost all teachers. It is part of the assessing of Advanced Skills Teachers (AST). The DfEE *Performance Management in Schools* (DfEE, June 2000) incorporates an annual review and target setting, and makes classroom observation part of the routine in schools. The model policy includes guidance on observation. Procedures in *Threshold Assessment* (DfEE, April 2000) make it clear that when the headteacher reviews the application, evidence from observation is a key factor in making the judgement about whether the teacher has met the standard relating to teaching.

1

Considering its importance and the very common perception that it is somehow threatening, it is perhaps surprising that few teachers have had any training in observation, or have even given it much thought. This may stem from the widespread assumption that we all know good teaching when we see it and to a certain extent this is true. What is more difficult is evaluating the quality of what we have seen and using this to help teachers identify and build on what is working well and what needs to be improved.

As with any other activity, there are skills to be learned. These include:

- planning the observation;

- agreeing a purpose;

- using the various methods;

- recording information;

- giving feedback both orally and in writing.

These and other issues are dealt with in detail in subsequent chapters. The starting point, however, is that teachers need to understand the reasons for undertaking observation. So why should teachers observe other teachers at work? The usual reasons given are professional development and accountability, and both of these need some exploration.

Professional and career development

Introducing appraisal into schools revealed that few teachers were able to identify clearly their professional development needs. Talking to teachers as part of OFSTED inspection indicates that many still find this difficult. Good teachers (and that means most teachers) are often their own severest critics. It is not unusual for an OFSTED inspector to reassure a teacher that the lesson he or she thought was a disaster was anything but. Teachers seldom have a clear idea about their strengths and weaknesses. This is often because they have not been systematically observed and constructively debriefed.

One of the most heartening developments in inspections has been the increasing emphasis on giving teachers feedback. It is relatively rare for a teacher to refuse the offer of a feedback session as most are only too pleased to have the opportunity to discuss their work. There may be some disagreements on the quality of what has been seen, but overwhelmingly teachers appreciate the analysis of strengths as well as any weaknesses. Many teachers, even those who are the most experienced and confident, may not be used to having their work praised on the basis of first-hand evidence. Experienced teachers can be surprised when their strengths are clearly identified; they may even think that what they do well is routine and not worthy of comment. However, praise and recognition are important for their self esteem and job satisfaction as well as encouraging their continued professional effectiveness.

A short meeting with an OFSTED inspector commenting on their class management or their questioning techniques may be the most objective view of their performance many teachers have had, albeit on the basis of only a few lessons. However useful, it is likely to happen only every four or five years. Think how much more effective regular observation and feedback could be from colleagues who can discuss work in greater depth, understand the school context, and are likely to be in a position to provide support and training in the future.

Development needs vary considerably at different times in a teacher's career. When we look at the scope of a teacher's job: long- and short-term planning; lesson preparation; choosing and using the best teaching methods for the activity; ensuring proper differentiation; assessing and marking work — to name but a few of the tasks — it is obvious that a newly qualified or inexperienced teacher is likely to need support. Scrutinising planning and marking will not give heads of department or mentors all the information they would find useful. However, the need to observe newly qualified teachers is rarely challenged. It is accepted as a necessary part of becoming a good teacher. Similarly teachers seeking promotion may need little convincing that being observed at work is justified. It is always easier to write a reference if we have seen someone teaching successfully.

More experienced teachers may well ask why they should be observed, since they are established and successful. However, even the experienced members of staff may need refresher courses from time to time to maintain their skills. Changes in requirements of the National Curriculum and public examinations, the introduction of new vocational courses, ensuring effective teaching for children with special educational needs or English as an additional language, all make demands on teachers. Just as the introduction of GCSE in the late 1980s forced many teachers to reappraise their teaching in Key Stages 3 and 4, the arrival of vocational courses has had a similar effect in sixth forms. Irrespective of external pressures, the school's own aims and priorities for development will have an impact on classroom practice. Sensitive and constructive observation which supports, but does not undermine, the confidence of the more experienced teachers can help them to identify their professional needs and cope more successfully with change whether externally imposed or generated through the school development plan.

Observing pastoral work

Pastoral work in school is another important area which can benefit. Schools invest a considerable amount of time and resources into tutor periods and PSHE. These lessons are often described as an integral part of the school's monitoring of academic development as well as being very important in terms of promoting pupils' personal development. Tutorial work will, in many schools, be the main means of teaching study skills, citizenship, health and drugs education, sex education, and sometimes even Religious Education (RE), yet teachers receive very little training in this aspect of their work on their PGCE or BEd course. Even individual interviews with parents and children can be observed, with suitable safeguards concerning confidentiality, and this is an area where feedback, other than the negative, is rare. We all know when an interview hasn't gone well, but how often do we analyse why one was successful? Observation can help pastoral staff to identify the successful techniques both in teaching and in interviews.

Observation of tutorial or PSHE lessons, when used with other techniques such as questionnaires and teachers' own evaluation, can be very helpful in evaluating the effectiveness of a tutorial programme for the pupils and in highlighting training needs for staff. Even schools where departmental lesson observation is routine do not always observe the tutorial programme. Tutorial work is often blocked on the timetable so that an entire year group is taught at the same time. Middle managers, such as heads of year or heads of house, frequently teach PSHE programmes and this makes it difficult for them to observe the work of their tutors unless the school plans for this.

 # Monitoring, evaluation and accountability

Accountability as a reason for observation can be more difficult for teachers to accept (despite, or possibly even because of, OFSTED inspections) but it is, and should be, a fact of professional life. Accountability, that is taking responsibility for what we are doing, should be an integral part of our approach to education. Just as schools expect their pupils to take responsibility for their own actions and work, so teachers too are accountable. The headteacher is accountable to governors for the management of the school, including the quality of teaching. The head of department is accountable for the quality of work in his or her subject, as is the head of year for the work in tutor groups. The subject teacher or tutor is responsible for the quality of his or her own work. Teachers at all levels should not see having to account for their work as a negative or punitive process, but as a means of analysing how well they are doing, getting praise and recognition for success and help where needed.

It is stating the obvious but it bears repeating that the long-term success of the school depends to a very great extent on the quality of teaching. Factors such as the nature of the intake, the size of the budget, the quality of accommodation, and the levels of resources are all significant and all contribute to a successful school. If, however, the teaching isn't as good as it could be, then the school is unlikely to give its pupils a good all-round education. It is hard to see how the headteacher and other managers in schools can be fully aware of the quality of work unless they are gaining first-hand information by systematically observing in classes. Making the right planning decisions about priorities for school development is easier if senior managers have recent and relevant information about the strengths and weaknesses of the teaching.

Systematic observation helps those with posts of responsibility to identify strengths and weaknesses in individuals and in the school as a whole. They are then in a position to spread good practice and help teachers learn from each other. Likewise, where weaknesses are identified, individuals can be supported and whole-school needs fed into the professional development programme.

There can also be unexpected benefits from observation. Teachers (and even OFSTED inspectors) who are experienced observers will agree that they often learn as much from the observation as the teacher does. In schools we often expect younger teachers to learn from observing the more experienced and perhaps forget that the reverse can also be true. It may be that the most recently qualified person in a department has skills that others don't have and these can and should be shared. Most of us might assume that the most obvious area is information and communication technology (ICT), but the clear identification of learning objectives and opportunities for assessment are also skills which recently qualified teachers can find it easier to articulate. Many effective departments are using 360° or reverse appraisal when teachers observe and give feedback about the work of their line manager. They recognise that the feedback on teaching and management is of value.

As well as ensuring accountability and good professional and career development, a well-structured and properly managed programme of observation can have a profound impact. It can lead to a more open climate, greater trust between colleagues, and the development of strong professional partnerships. The recognition that all teachers face the same challenges and can learn from each other can be of great benefit in boosting and maintaining staff morale.

 ## School commitment

Making all this happen requires a commitment from the governors and senior management of the school to invest the necessary time and resources. Classroom observation should be part of routine monitoring. Where a school or department has a more specific need, such as evaluating the impact of whole school in-service training or the implementation of a departmental or whole-school policy, this can be done as part of the normal schedule and provide the focus for the observation. A senior member of staff has to have responsibility for implementing and monitoring the programme. Time and resources must be carefully costed, a manageable schedule worked out and, above all, the outcomes must be taken seriously. Staff time and energy are too precious to waste on a programme which is not carried out systematically and does not meet the staff and school needs.

2 Approaches to lesson observation: matching the type of observation to the purpose

Observation can take a number of different forms, but there are two broad categories:

- **general** or **whole-class**

- **focused**, where the observer concentrates on a specific aspect of the lesson or specific pupils.

General observation

Let us look first at the stereotype of general observation, which is the one most people think of if they think about observation at all. The observer is a 'fly on the wall' sitting at the back or in a corner of the room with a clipboard, if not also a stop watch, observing and making notes on everything that happens in the room. (If the observer is external to the school, for example an LEA or an OFSTED inspector, then it will probably be assumed that he is a man in a grey suit as well!) The teacher and the class are put under a microscope. Nothing and no-one escapes the observer's eagle eye. Like most stereotypes this contains grains of truth, but is far from being the whole story.

In a general observation, you as the observer try to see the lesson as a whole. You need to look at the structure of the lesson and how the various sections fit together, the planning, the response of pupils, the way in which resources are used. You are likely to be looking at the overall effectiveness of the teaching, answering the question, 'What impact is the teaching having on the attainment and progress of the pupils?' or, put another way, 'What have the pupils achieved?' All teachers want to make sure that their pupils are making as much progress as possible. You should be able to use the observation to evaluate the strengths and weaknesses in the teaching.

Evaluating the impact of teaching on attainment is relatively straightforward. The National Curriculum and, where relevant, examination syllabuses, provide information about expectations at different stages. The level descriptors for most subjects and the end of key stage statements for citizenship describe what most pupils should know, understand and be able to do at different stages. While open to interpretation, these do at least give you as an observer some benchmarks.

You should be able to see the level at which the work is pitched from the planning, even if it is not expressed in terms of a National Curriculum level or an attainment target. The planning should also indicate whether the teacher has taken account of special educational needs and, where relevant, of the needs of pupils with English as an additional language.

The response of the class should indicate whether the work has been pitched at a level that is about right, or too easy or difficult for most pupils. The nature of the questions pupils ask, as well as behaviour and attitudes, are clues. In the course of the observation, make sure you look at the range of attainment in the class. Does the work cater for this range? How effective is the differentiation? Try to estimate what proportion of pupils are working at different levels. This is also helpful in evaluating the effectiveness of the teaching and is useful feedback.

The impact of teaching on learning, and therefore progress, is harder to evaluate in the context of one lesson. A sparkling lesson from the obviously charismatic teacher may well be having the major impact you expect. Be careful, though, not to be so impressed by the 'firework display' from a teacher that you don't look in depth at what pupils can do. The pupils may appear to be fully engaged in that they are enjoying the performance, but may not actually learn a great deal. A teacher with a quieter style may in fact be as or more effective and thorough. Encouraging reflective learning is as important for a teacher as encouraging active learning.

Talking to pupils, and noting from the questions they ask how confident they are, will help you to establish their progress more securely both in the lesson and over a period of time. You will need to look at what they know as well as how their level of skills and understanding are developing. Looking at their books during and possibly after the lesson will help to establish what they have learned. Not all lessons, however, will introduce new work and so you are very likely to be looking for evidence of good consolidation and reinforcement of knowledge, skills and understanding. Not just 'What do they know about the Norman Conquest or photosynthesis or six-figure co-ordinates that they didn't know at the start of the lesson?' as 'How much better is their understanding and ability to use the information'.

When evaluating what you are seeing and gauging progress over time, you can and should draw on your own knowledge of the work of the department, year group or the school as a whole. You should be aware of the requirements of the schemes of work or examination syllabus. If not a specialist, you should at least have made yourself familiar with the subject requirements.

This general approach can be used with individual teachers as a starting point for discussion and further observation. Its use with newly qualified teachers is common, but it is also a profitable approach with more experienced staff. A new headteacher or head of department could use this approach to establish personal benchmarks as well as using it as a means of getting to know the staff and pupils. When systematically introduced into schools where observation has not been part of the routine, it is a useful way of establishing a baseline for the quality of teaching in the school as a whole and in identifying whole-school issues for training and development.

The advantages of the general approach are clear:

■ It gives you and the teacher a good general view of a whole range of issues. These include the effectiveness of teaching strategies, class organisation and management, discipline and relationships, the quality of planning and preparation.

■ It is a particularly good way of assessing pupils' overall response.

■ You are likely to notice things which the teacher may be unaware of, both strengths and weaknesses. Teachers are not always really aware of their strengths or take them for granted, assuming that everyone is as good as they are.

■ It provides useful information as a starting point for further, more focused, observation and for discussion.

■ A lesson is more than the sum of the individual parts and evaluating its overall impact can help to evaluate the effectiveness of whole-school policies and procedures.

The general approach has its disadvantages as well:

■ If what is recorded is too descriptive and not evaluative, it becomes a superficial exercise which gives little useful information.

■ It can be difficult to reach conclusions about what pupils are actually learning unless you are able to talk to them.

■ It is not always easy to gauge the effectiveness of the differentiation, particularly if it is by outcome, or through support.

■ You can't see everything. The observer is in the position of a camera; you can only record what you actually see and in choosing to look in one direction you may miss other things that are important.

When doing this sort of observation, you will need to ask yourself key questions about the teacher's skills such as:

■ How secure is the teacher's subject knowledge?

■ Is the teacher using school routines consistently and effectively?

■ What is the teacher hoping to achieve and what did he or she achieve?

■ Does the work match the range of ability in the class?

■ Is the teacher expecting the highest possible standards of work and behaviour from all pupils?

■ Does the work keep the pupils fully and profitably occupied?

■ Is the teacher asking challenging questions which really move pupils on?

■ What did the pupils actually learn?

Issues of classroom organisation and management are also important. Is the room well organised and used to maximum advantage? The teacher may have little control over the layout, the availability of display, the storage or lack of it, but is he or she making the best use of what there is? It is not uncommon, for example, if tables are arranged in groups, to see an inexperienced teacher trying to talk to the whole class, some of whom may have their backs to him or her, where a more experienced teacher would quickly have rearranged the seating. If pupils need specific resources, are these easily accessible and are there enough? Is it easy to get access to ICT equipment? If the teacher has sole use of the classroom, is the display relevant and attractive? Is the classroom clean and tidy; are pupils expected to tidy up? If the problems are beyond the teacher's control, then the evidence of your observation can be helpful in raising issues with senior management.

In this type of observation, it is sensible to try to stay for the full session. This enables you to see the start and finish of the lesson and the transition between activities. The importance of a good start is obvious. The ability to settle the class quickly, a link with what has gone before, a quick warm-up question and answer session, a clear explanation of what this lesson is going to be about are all points to look for. Most teachers appreciate the significance of a review and summing up. This often includes a question-and-answer session, comment or feedback from pupils about what they have learned, and a brief comment which indicates what will be happening in the next lesson. The manner in which the class is sent on its way is also significant.

The comments you make about how well the lesson started or finished should be useful to the teacher and open up opportunities for discussion. Look for and note the positive points. For example, in a mathematics lesson you might note that the questions in the mental maths session at the beginning were well targeted to test the range of attainment and that virtually everyone was willing to 'have a go'. You might also compare the differences between the response of different groups to a plenary session. For example, a discussion about why one group found the presentation harder than the others might help the teacher see how a slight change in the instructions given could raise their achievement.

A difficult area for some teachers is making the transition from one part of the lesson to another. This is a point where pupils can be distracted, attention can wander and those with a tendency to be disruptive get the opportunity. If you watch the whole of the lesson this will enable you to help the teacher to identify where the pace slips or explanations are not clear enough to allow pupils to get on easily. Did it simply take too long to give out the resources needed? Were the resources not well-prepared? Were the instructions, whether oral or written, clear enough to allow all groups to get started quickly? Were support staff well briefed so that they could help their group or groups to settle to work quickly?

Specific focus for observation

A focused observation concentrates on a specific aspect of teaching or learning. This can relate to the class as a whole, to groups or individuals or to other aspects such as the deployment of support staff, the use of resources, or pastoral interviews between staff and pupils and/or parents. The focus can arise from an analysis of previous observations or the teacher's own lesson evaluation. If you are a head of department, it might stem from your routine monitoring of planning or marking. It could come from a whole-school focus; for example many schools are looking closely at the attainment of boys or the use of ICT. It might arise from the observation of the pastoral work of the school. As for general observation, it is helpful to have a prompt list for the observation, but this could be selected from the prompt list for a general observation and tailored specifically for the focus.

Whole class

Examples of focused whole-class observation could include questioning techniques, the participation of boys or girls or different ethnic groups, the effectiveness of time management, group dynamics within the class.

- Analysing questioning techniques can help teachers to see how they could be more challenging in using probing questions to check and extend pupils' understanding. It can also indicate whether the teacher is working more effectively with boys or girls or with pupils of differing attainment in the class.

- Keeping a time log when observing can help the teacher to see where slippage is happening, where the pace might be brisker and how to improve the all-important transitions from one part of the lesson to the next.

- Evaluating the response and the contribution of boys and girls can help to identify where specific action is needed in relation to one or the other group.

- The appropriateness of the choice of study materials, including textbooks and other learning resources, should be evaluated, as should their availability, how they are woven into the lesson, and the teacher's supportive guidance on the reading of text and diagrams in the use of a textbook.

The main advantages of this approach are that it enables you to concentrate on a more limited aspect of the teaching and learning and not be concerned about what you might be missing. You are in a position to give detailed feedback to the teacher on an aspect of teaching that you have both agreed is important. The main disadvantage is that in certain types of specific focus, for example time management, it can be difficult to reach conclusions about what pupils are actually learning and it would not be easy to make judgements on the effectiveness of differentiation. It is easier to record the mechanics of teaching than it is to evaluate its impact.

Group

An observation with a group focus would normally involve the observer in working with one group of pupils, observing their response to the lesson and evaluating what they are doing. This is often used to look at the provision for and response of pupils with special educational needs (SEN) or English as an additional language (EAL), but it can be equally well used with a mixed-ability group or a group of higher attainers. This approach also enables you to concentrate on a more limited aspect of the teaching and learning.

You can focus very closely on the progress of the group by discussing with them what they are doing and how they are approaching it, as well as by looking at their work with them. Pupils are usually only too willing to talk about what they are doing and are, more often than not, thoughtful and sensible in their responses. Some may at times seem flippant but this is usually only superficial. You are likely to know many of the pupils and may indeed have taught them yourself, so it should be possible to get below the surface quite quickly.

Focusing on a group enables you to reach more secure judgements about the match of work to the ability/attainment of that group of pupils. Is the work pitched at a suitable level? Is it sufficiently difficult to challenge the pupils and make them think, but not so hard that they become frustrated or discouraged? Is the language of every worksheet pitched at an appropriate level for the intended students? Is any difficult or specialist vocabulary explained?

The main disadvantage of this approach is that too close a focus on a group may distort your view of the effectiveness of the teaching for the class as a whole, and you may lose sight of the context and overall aims of the lesson.

Individual

An individual focus could be to track a pupil for a specific period of time such as a morning or, if time permits, a whole day, to see what sort of experience the pupil has and how well the work is matched to his or her needs. This has the additional advantage of providing a great deal of information about the quality of teaching and the implementation of whole-school policies in different classes and subjects.

It can be a salutary experience to find out exactly what a day in the life of a pupil is like. One tracking exercise revealed that a particular pupil had not been directly addressed by a teacher for an entire day. Another exercise was useful in evaluating the impact of the use of supply teachers and the effectiveness of the school's briefing procedures. The main disadvantages of the individual focus are, as with the observation of a group, that it is easy to lose sight of the overall context of the lesson and the impact of the teaching on the majority of pupils.

As shown, each of these types of observation has advantages and can be used very effectively, but each also has its disadvantages. Observers and teachers need therefore to consider very carefully the purpose of an observation to make sure that they agree the best approach and select the most appropriate type of observation.

▨ Observing newly qualified and beginning teachers

The Teacher Training Agency (TTA) guidance for the induction year for newly qualified teachers (NQTs) is very specific about the need for the NQT to be observed once every half term. The observation, normally by the teacher's mentor or another senior member of staff or LEA adviser, is expected to relate to the teacher's entry profile and the targets set in that. The aim of observation of NQTs is to help them to become confident and skilled teachers. The information gleaned from observation should help them to build on and put into practice the knowledge and skills they bring from their PGCE or BEd course and develop other areas where they may not be so confident.

The purpose of observation in these circumstances is very specific and should always result in the targets being agreed or refined. The mentor needs to be fully aware of these targets and discuss and agree in advance of the lesson what the specific focus should be. Giving direct advice is therefore an important part of this type of observation. The observer should be prepared to make clear suggestions about what the teacher can do to improve the quality of planning and delivery.

The record of the observation forms part of the portfolio of evidence, which will determine whether the NQT successfully completes his or her induction year. One observation should therefore follow logically on from and build on the previous one. The observations should be seen as an integral part of the induction programme, which also normally includes meetings about specific issues, regular review meetings and target setting, observation of other staff, visits to other schools, and/or participation in an LEA programme.

Beginning teachers are likely to be observed by a range of people: their tutors, staff in the department whose classes they are teaching and, in many schools, professional tutors. It is important that beginning teachers get a consistent message and that the school works closely with the training institution as well as adhering to its own policies. As with NQTs, beginning teachers will need quite explicit advice and guidance, including the setting of targets. The school staff will, of course, recognise that beginning teachers are less experienced than the newly qualified and will need more support and help with preparation.

Observation by NQTs and beginning teachers

An NQT or a beginning teacher observing more experienced teachers will need to prepare. Understanding the context of the lesson is very important. The NQT needs to know how the lesson to be observed fits into a sequence, what level the majority of the class are working at, any particular features about the class and setting/grouping arrangements. The beginning teacher needs to know as much as possible about the school as well as the context of the actual lesson.

Discussion about what was observed is important. This is a means of identifying techniques which might be appropriate for the NQT or beginning teacher as well as those which he or she might not yet be experienced enough to use. We all have our idiosyncrasies as teachers, which might not be helpful for a new teacher to copy.

When an NQT is observing, it is helpful if he or she has a checklist to enable him/her to analyse class-management skills being used successfully. Interesting material and stimulating tasks pitched at the right level do not of themselves guarantee successful lessons. How does the teacher greet pupils at the beginning of the lesson to establish a good atmosphere? What is it about the way in which the lesson starts that ensures a brisk pace? How does he or she deal with any latecomers? How does the teacher make sure that all pupils are fully involved? How are resources given out without loss of momentum? How does the teacher prevent or, if necessary, deal with minor irritations/low level disruption which could impede the progress of other pupils? What does the teacher do to dismiss the pupils to ensure that they move on to the next lesson in a purposeful way? In this way the observation should focus on what the teacher is doing which works rather than individual mannerisms, and the NQT can then think about how to apply the techniques in the classroom.

3 Criteria for making judgements about teaching

It is essential that observation takes place in the context of agreed criteria on effective teaching. It helps the individual teacher by making expectations explicit and it helps the school by promoting consistency. It does not mean a boring uniformity nor that somehow teachers will become 'clones'. Teaching, because it is essentially founded on relationships, cannot be defined in terms of a set of activities or actions that will always work in any circumstances. It can, however, be defined in terms of expectations. We *expect* teachers to have appropriate subject knowledge, to plan the work, to take account of what pupils already know, etc. These expectations have been set out by the DfEE as part of the *Performance Management in Schools* (DfEE, June 2000) and *Threshold Assessment* (DfEE, April 2000). The national standards for qualified teacher status (QTS) and for induction from the Teacher Training Agency (National Standards 1998) provide a similar basis for observing the work of newly qualified teachers, and OFSTED provides guidance for its inspectors (OFSTED *Handbook* and *Framework for Inspection*, January 2000).

Developing agreed criteria

Many schools have already discovered that observation is valid and more useful if, as a school or department, they have agreed a set of broad criteria which can be applied to any subject. Such criteria are useful as a prompt list when observing and making notes. You would, of course, not expect to see all of your criteria fulfilled in any one lesson. Schools might choose to devise their own or take the published criteria as they stand or adapt them to suit their particular circumstances. For example, the headings of the TTA national induction standards translated into a policy might look like this:

■ School-developed criteria

A   Knowledge and understanding

Subject knowledge

■ Does the teacher have a good knowledge of the subject, including the requirements of the National Curriculum and any examination syllabuses?

B   Planning, teaching and class management

Expectations

■ Does the teacher have a good knowledge of the levels at which pupils are already working?

■ Is the level of challenge high enough for all pupils?

■ Is there an emphasis on pupils working hard and accurately, and presenting their work well?

■ Are pupils learning to criticise their own work constructively and to be creative and imaginative?

Planning

■ Are teaching strategies identified in the planning?

■ Is the planning meeting the needs of the range in the class?

■ Are objectives for lessons clear?

■ Does the planning indicate how any support staff will be briefed and deployed?

■ Are links with previous work clear?

■ Are requirements of the National Curriculum clearly indicated in planning?

■ Are assessment opportunities identified in planning?

Teaching methods

■ Is the introduction brisk, does it share aims and objectives for the lesson with pupils?

■ Are methods appropriate to the work, e.g. whole class, group, paired, individual?

■ Are instructions given clearly and precisely?

■ Is the teaching style right for the content, e.g. oral, written, practical, problem solving, discussion, explanation/exposition, demonstration?

■ Does the teaching style help to motivate pupils?

■ Does the teacher make effective use of voice, humour, challenging questions, feedback, the board/flipchart/OHP?

■ Is the teacher able to deal with the unexpected, e.g. using the questions pupils ask?

■ How good is the match between planning and delivery?

■ Is there an effective summary reminding pupils of what they should have learned and giving a brief indication of what it is leading on to?

Classroom organisation
- Is the classroom well organised and tidy?
- Is the layout appropriate to the style of lessons?
- Are resources readily accessible to teacher and pupils?
- Are resources well chosen to support the work?
- Are displays relevant?
- Are displays used effectively?
- Are pupils given responsibility for keeping the classroom neat and tidy?

Discipline and behaviour management
- Are relationships good?
- Are the school expectations for behaviour understood?
- Are rewards and sanctions policies clearly and consistently implemented?
- Does the teacher follow school policies, e.g. taking a register, dealing with latecomers, setting homework?
- Is the teacher encouraging pupils to be self-disciplined?
- Is the classroom orderly, with a good working atmosphere?

C   Monitoring, assessment

Monitoring
- Is the teacher monitoring and evaluating the success of lessons?
- Is the teacher setting targets with pupils?

Assessment
- How well do teachers use praise and/or encouragement, and take advantage of mistakes or misconceptions in class to extend and improve pupils' knowledge and understanding?
- Is assessment being used to identify individual needs and to inform planning?
- Does teacher assessment and pupils' self-assessment help improve performance?
- Is pupils' work marked regularly and helpfully, and does the marking identify what pupils need to do to improve?
- Does the assessment of pupils with special educational needs relate closely to the requirements of the IEPs?
- Is homework set in line with policy, and does it reinforce and extend work in school?

D   Other professional requirements
- Is the teacher making use of ICT?
- Does the teacher have access to appropriate support and training?

Criteria for observing NQTs

Schools and LEAs have devised approaches to observing NQTs based on the national standards. The criteria for observation used at Addington High School in Croydon were developed specifically for use with NQTs. They provide the mentor with a series of prompts related to headings on an observation form. This is useful to the individual mentor, and helps to ensure consistency across the school, which is vital.

ADDINGTON HIGH SCHOOL:
NQT LESSON OBSERVATION PROMPTS

Planning and preparation

- clear aims and objectives
- match to National Curriculum faculty scheme of work
- match of content to ability range
- differentiation
- progression and continuity
- recognition of SEN in group
- selection of a variety of tasks and methods
- well-prepared selection of resources
- awareness of equal opportunities issues
- homework: setting and sensitivity to pupils' backgrounds

Subject expertise

- command of knowledge required
- steps taken to fill in gaps in knowledge

Classroom management

- punctual start: controlled entry
- handling of latecomers/interruptions
- suitable clear start to lesson
- appropriate taking of register
- immediacy: getting into tasks
- distribution and collection of materials
- handling of inappropriate behaviours with a range of strategies
- clarity, focus and appropriateness of reprimand
- awareness of value of non-confrontational strategies
- timing of clearing up
- punctual, orderly departure

Management of learning activities

- clearly stated aims and introduction
- sensible pace and timing of lesson
- balance of activity: exposition, discussion, practical etc
- communication of instructions which are clear and appropriate to ability
- setting of deadlines
- anticipation of difficulties
- handling of the transition of activities
- selection and organisation for learning task
- setting of differentiated tasks/outcomes
- identification and summary of learning

Pupil learning

- objectives achieved
- lesson an enjoyable experience
- quality of learning: relevance to faculty scheme of work and to pupils
- learning at appropriate level: stretched, not trivial
- appropriate monitoring of learning
- identification and summary of learning

Assessment skills

- relevant homework
- marking and assessment in line with school policy
- formative comments

Classroom presence

- positive presence
- body language, facial expressions
- eye contact
- appropriate means of communication, properly used
- voice: pace, pitch, clarity
- appropriate vocabulary
- confident manner and clear sense of purpose
- confident movement around the classroom
- sense of professional role
- aware of need to set boundaries
- alert, 'with it', using common sense,

DfEE Performance Management guidance

Another approach would be to take that of the DfEE in *Performance Management in Schools* (DfEE, June 2000). A major piece of research, commissioned by the DfEE and carried out by Hay McBer, into the characteristics of effective teaching is the foundation for the whole Performance Management Framework. (Hay McBer, *Research into Teacher Effectiveness* – a report to the DfEE, June 2000.) The main findings of the report can be found in the Appendix. The model identifies three key areas:

1. **professional characteristics;**
2. **teaching skills;**
3. **classroom climate.**

The **professional characteristics** are broken down into a number of clusters:

Professionalism
■ respect for others;

■ challenge and support;

■ confidence;

■ creating trust.

Thinking
■ analytical thinking;

■ conceptual thinking.

Planning and setting expectations
■ drive for improvement;

■ initiative;

■ information seeking.

Leading
■ managing pupils;

■ passion for learning;

■ flexibility;

■ holding people accountable.

Relating to others

■ understanding others;

■ impact and influence;

■ teamworking.

Each aspect of these is then further defined. The clusters and the definitions are not intended to provide a blueprint or template for effective teaching. The research showed that strength in each cluster is important, but not necessarily in the same depth or combination. Different combinations can work equally well.

The lesson observation guidance in the *Performance Management Framework* (DfEE, June 2000) is derived from the section in the Hay McBer research on teaching skills. It identifies eight key areas:

1. **The teacher plans effectively and sets clear objectives that are understood.**
■ Objectives are communicated clearly at the start of the lesson.
■ Materials are ready.
■ There is a good structure to the lesson.
■ The lesson is reviewed at the end.
■ The learning needs of those with IEPs are incorporated with the teacher's planning.

2. **The teacher shows good subject knowledge and understanding.**
■ The teacher has a thorough knowledge of the subject content covered in the lesson.
■ The subject material is appropriate for the lesson.
■ Knowledge is made relevant and interesting for pupils.

3. **The teaching methods used enable all pupils to learn effectively.**
■ The lesson is linked to previous teaching or learning.
■ The ideas and experiences of pupils are drawn upon.
■ A variety of activities and questioning techniques is used.
■ Instructions and explanations are clear and specific.
■ The teacher involves all pupils, listens to them and responds appropriately.
■ High standards of effort, accuracy and presentation are encouraged.
■ Appropriate methods of differentiation are used.

4. **Pupils are well managed and high standards of behaviour are insisted upon.**
- Pupils are praised regularly for their good effort and achievement.
- Prompt action is taken to address poor behaviour.
- All pupils are treated fairly, with an equal emphasis on the work of boys and girls and all ability groups.

5. **Pupils' work is assessed thoroughly.**
- Pupil understanding is assessed throughout the lesson by the use of the teacher's questions.
- Mistakes and misconceptions are recognised by the teacher and used constructively to facilitate learning.
- Pupils' written work is assessed regularly and accurately.

6. **Pupils achieve productive outcomes.**
- Pupils remain fully engaged throughout the lesson and make progress in the lesson.
- Pupils understand what work is expected of them during the lesson.
- The pupil outcomes of the lesson are consistent with the objectives set at the beginning.
- The teacher and pupils work at a good pace.

7. **The teacher makes effective use of time and resources.**
- Time is well utilised and learning is maintained for the full time available.
- A good pace is maintained throughout the lesson.
- Good use is made of any support available, e.g. learning assistants and older pupils.
- Appropriate learning resources are used, e.g. ICT.

8. **Homework is used effectively to reinforce and extend learning.**
- Homework is set, if appropriate.
- Learning objectives are explicit and relate to the work in progress.
- Homework is followed up if it has been set previously.

The DfEE 'Lesson Observation: Summative Assessment' form (see Chapter 6) has eight corresponding sections and the expectation is that most, if not all, should apply to any lesson. The observer considers for each aspect whether it has been shown to an excellent standard, a good standard, a satisfactory standard; whether further development is needed; or whether the aspect is not applicable or there is not enough evidence to assess it. The DfEE guidance is very clear that conclusions should always be supported by evidence.

OFSTED guidelines

The OFSTED guidance is written for the benefit of OFSTED inspectors who are required to evaluate and judge the quality of teaching in terms of its impact on learning and what features make it successful or not. It is designed to ensure that inspectors make their judgements against published criteria and that there is as high a degree of consistency as possible in the judgements made by different inspectors. The OFSTED list of criteria is relatively short but in its essence it is very similar to those of the DfEE and the TTA. OFSTED is very clear about the absolute essentials.

The criteria are supported by a more detailed analysis of the constituents of good teaching in the OFSTED *Handbook for Inspecting Secondary Schools* (January 2000, pp. 44–57). These expand on the basic statement and link the elements of teaching very explicitly with their impact on pupils' learning. The quality of teaching should be judged by the extent to which the teachers:

- show good subject knowledge and understanding in the way they present and discuss their subject;

- are technically competent in teaching basic skills;

- plan effectively, setting clear objectives that pupils understand;

- challenge and inspire pupils, expecting the most of them, so as to deepen their knowledge and understanding;

- use methods which enable all pupils to learn effectively;

- manage pupils well and insist on high standards of behaviour;

- use time, support staff and other resources, especially information and communications technology, effectively;

- assess pupils' work thoroughly and use assessments to help and encourage pupils to overcome difficulties;

- use homework effectively to reinforce and/or extend what is learned in school.

The teaching must be evaluated in terms of the extent to which pupils and students:

- acquire new knowledge or skills, develop ideas and increase their understanding;

- apply intellectual, physical or creative effort in their work;

- are productive and work at a good pace;

- show interest in their work, are able to sustain concentration and think and learn for themselves;

- understand what they are doing, how well they have done and how they can improve.

In guiding inspectors in making their judgements, OFSTED is very explicit about the absolute minimum required. Teaching cannot be satisfactory if any one of the following is present:

- teachers' knowledge of subjects is not good enough to promote demanding work;

- basic skills are not taught effectively;

- a significant minority of pupils are not engaged in the lesson;

- lessons are poorly planned and organised and time is wasted;

- there are weaknesses in controlling the class;

- pupils do not know what they are doing;

- pupils are not making progress.

This may seem like a deficit model of teaching, but in practice teachers would not disagree with these points and the rest of the guidance is couched in positive terms.

Threshold standards

The threshold standards set out in *Threshold Assessment* (DfEE, April 2000) set out what the expectations are for experienced teachers. In applying for the threshold payment, teachers are expected to demonstrate their competence across all aspects of the job.

Knowledge and understanding:

Teachers should demonstrate that they have a thorough and up-to-date knowledge of the teaching of their subject(s) and take account of wider curriculum developments which are relevant to their work.

Teaching and assessment:

Teachers should demonstrate that they consistently and effectively:

- plan lessons and sequences of lessons to meet pupils' individual learning needs;

- use a range of appropriate strategies for teaching and classroom management;

- use information about prior attainment to set well-grounded expectations for pupils, and monitor progress to give clear and constructive feedback.

Pupil progress:

Teachers should demonstrate that, as a result of their teaching, their pupils achieve well relative to the pupils' prior attainment, making progress as good or better than similar pupils nationally. This should be shown in marks or grades in any relevant national tests or examinations, or school-based assessment for pupils where national tests and examinations are not taken.

Wider professional effectiveness:

Teachers should demonstrate that they:

- take responsibility for their professional development and use the outcomes to improve their teaching and pupils' learning;

- make an active contribution to the policies and aspirations of the school.

Professional characteristics:

Teachers should demonstrate that they are effective professionals who challenge and support all pupils to do their best through:

- inspiring trust and confidence;

- building team commitment;

- engaging and motivating pupils;

- analytical thinking;

- positive action to improve the quality of pupils' learning.

The five standards are interlinked and the evidence is expected to be consistent across the standards. The guidance on applying for the threshold payment expands the criteria to describe the expectations in relation to classroom observation, and this could form the basis of school criteria. The group of standards relating to teaching and assessment seeks evidence that teachers:

Consistently and effectively plan lessons and sequences of lessons to meet pupils' individual learning needs

For example by:

■ using their knowledge of pupils' learning needs to plan lessons and sequences of lessons, to target individuals and groups effectively and to ensure good year-on-year progression;

■ communicating learning objectives clearly to pupils;

■ making effective use of homework and other opportunities for learning outside the classroom.

Consistently and effectively use a range of appropriate strategies for teaching and classroom management

For example by:

■ understanding and applying the most effective lesson structures, classroom organisation and teaching strategies and methods appropriate to motivate different pupils and groups of pupils;

■ providing positive and targeted support for any pupils with particular learning needs, maintaining high levels of behaviour and discipline and dealing promptly and effectively with misbehaviour and bullying;

■ managing efficiently and creatively the time and the full range of resources available for pupils' learning, including, as appropriate, adults other than teachers.

Consistently and effectively use information about prior attainment to set well-grounded expectations for pupils and monitor progress to give clear and constructive feedback

For example by:

■ evaluating pupils' progress in relation to national, local and school targets and setting realistic and challenging targets for improvement;

■ using assessment as part of everyday teaching to monitor pupils' progress and adapting teaching approaches as necessary to provide more support;

■ reporting clearly and in detail to pupils, parents and to the head-teacher and team leader as required on progress achieved and action required.

Whichever method a school chooses – whether 'home grown' or taken from the DfEE, the TTA or OFSTED documents – staff must understand the significance of the criteria and how they will be applied. If staff are to accept observation as fair and helpful, the importance of consistency of application cannot be over-emphasised.

4 Planning and preparation: the basis of success

If observation is to be useful, then everyone involved has to have a very clear idea of why it is being done, what form the observation will take, and what follow-up there will be. What do you both expect to learn? A degree of joint preparation is therefore not just desirable, it is essential.

The new regulations for the employment of newly qualified teachers (NQTs) provide for them to have a mentor as part of their induction. A more senior member of staff takes specific responsibility for the new teacher and is required to observe his or her work in the classroom and to give advice and support as necessary. As a starting point, both mentor and NQT must be familiar with the school's policy for induction. It would not be unusual for the NQT to know more about this than the mentor, unless of course the mentor has whole-school responsibility for the induction programme. As mentor, therefore, you must read the policy carefully, know how many observations are required and at what intervals. You must know the expectations for feedback, and when and to whom written reports should be submitted.

For more experienced teachers, performance management, threshold assessment, and Advanced Skills Teachers (AST) status all assume an element of observation. This may be set up for a specific purpose, as, for example, when a teacher applies to be an AST and must be externally assessed. For the purposes of performance management and threshold assessment, however, the observations are likely to be part of the normal routine pattern of monitoring and evaluation. There are strong arguments for not undertaking separate exercises solely for the purpose of satisfying a performance management policy as it then tends to become a 'bolt-on' exercise and not integrated into the school routine. Whatever the purpose of the exercise, teachers need to have a clear understanding of the importance of their own contribution to successful and therefore helpful observation.

Choice of lessons

Whether you are observing an NQT or an experienced teacher, the first observation is likely to be of a general nature. As the observer, you should discuss the class to be observed. It is usually better to give the teacher some choice in this, particularly when mentoring an NQT. Initially it is more productive to observe teachers with classes where they feel confident. As an NQT, being watched teaching the most challenging class early in one's first term may not raise morale or help to develop teaching skills. Difficult classes must not be ignored, but could come later. Teachers may also need to develop confidence in the process. It may not be possible to give the teacher a choice of lessons because of a whole-school focus for observation or timetabling constraints. In this case you must explain why.

Practical arrangements

First consider the practical details, which are very important to the success or otherwise of the observation. You must make sure that you both know where and when the lesson will take place. You should also make sure that there will be a chair for you. This may sound very obvious but it is surprising how often an observer is stranded in the doorway looking for somewhere to sit down. This has the effect of drawing attention to you, which is not what you want to achieve. It is also helpful if you can have instant access to planning.

The observer should know the context of the lesson and be aware of any organisational issues. Is this a set (if so, at what level?); is it mixed ability, is it an examination class? You may not think this is necessary because, as a more senior member of staff, you should understand the school's grouping policy and know the distribution of classes to staff within the subject. You would be wise, though, to check on this and, if you are not directly responsible for that teacher's work, you may need some more detail. You cannot do justice to the teacher without this sort of information. The teacher should also consider what needs to be said to the class, as pupils may well ask why another teacher is present.

For all lessons, you must ask for specific information about the content and the teacher's expectations. A copy of a lesson plan which gives brief information about learning objectives, special needs, and English as an additional language, as well as particular factors, is essential. For example, is this an introductory lesson or the middle or end of a series? It could be helpful, too, for the teacher and the observer to complete a brief observation planning sheet. Both the observer and the teacher should have a copy, but this should not be seen as a substitute for the lesson plan. It is also important to avoid turning the process into a bureaucratic paper-chase. A planning sheet might look like the one below.

If you do not have this sort of information, whether in a separate form or as a lesson plan, you may well find yourself making false assumptions about what you are seeing. If you are watching a lesson where there is little initial explanation of what seem to you to be key points, it may well be that these have been thoroughly covered in previous lessons. If you had known in advance that this was the third lesson in a sequence, it would not be unreasonable to assume that the explanations had already been made. When talking to pupils, you might then focus on what they have understood of previous lessons.

If there is time, you might find it helpful to look in advance at some samples of work, though this may already be part of routine monitoring and you should not duplicate effort. If you do want to look at work, the teacher needs to know when you will want the work, how much and at what level of ability.

Observation Planning Sheet

Teacher: Observer:
Subject and group: Date and time:
Room: Length of observation:
Time and place of feedback:

Context of lesson
(e.g. content, NC/exam levels, class
organisation, teaching approach,
position in sequence of lessons)

Purpose of observation
(e.g. NQT, HoD monitoring, pupil
tracking)

Specific issues
(e.g. SEN, EAL)

**Type/specific purpose of
observation**
(e.g. whole class, group, SEN,
attainment of boys, use of ICT)

Agreeing the purpose

The specific purpose of an observation should be clear to both the observer and the teacher. The specific purpose could be determined by whole-school, department, or year group considerations. For example, in a school where the attainment of boys is high on the school's priority list, observations whether general, focused or individual are likely to concentrate on that area in particular, whereas another school might have evaluating the success of its literacy or numeracy policy as a priority. The integration of pupils with special educational needs and the use of individual education plans (IEPs) could be another whole-school example. Partnership teaching in relation to bilingual learners is another area which a school might choose to evaluate through observation.

Within a department, you may be looking at a particular aspect of work. Some examples of a particular aspect could be AT1 in Mathematics or Science, or the use of evidence in History, or the relationship of the design aspect of Design and Technology to the making aspect. As a year head, you might want to look at the response to a particular feature of the PSHE programme, such as Year 9 options or university entrance and UCAS forms. The possibilities for a specific purpose are considerable, and when determining these you should refer to the current school and/or subject development plan.

It is likely that some observations will be determined by the specific needs of individual teachers, perhaps arising from a general observation, perhaps from OFSTED, or from an appraisal discussion. It could, however, quite simply be a request for guidance where the teacher feels that he or she needs the benefit of advice from someone more experienced. This needs a degree of trust because, in the past, such a request was too often seen as an admission of failure.

Teachers are still likely to be reluctant to ask for this type of observation if they are concerned that they will be judged unable to cope. They might feel that at some time it will affect a threshold payment. However, a number of teachers are aware that they lack the ICT skills they increasingly need and this could be a route into creating a climate where teachers are not as worried about admitting to being less than perfect. As already said, ICT is also often a means whereby less experienced teachers who have specific skills can observe and advise their more experienced colleagues.

▰ School policy

Schools embarking on a programme of observation for the first time would be wise to consider the implications, and produce a policy statement and a brief set of guidelines relating to the conduct of the observer. These guidelines do need reviewing and revising in the light of experience. (For an outline policy see Chapter 10.) The policy must be consistent with any statutory requirements such as the management of NQTs or teacher appraisal. A Code of Conduct for observers is advisable. (For a draft code see Chapter 10.)

Remember that you are a visitor in someone else's classroom. You should not do anything which undermines that teacher. He or she must make decisions about what the pupils do. Most of the time the pupils will be sensible and not react adversely to your presence, though they may be quieter than usual to start with. However, pupils can respond in unexpected ways and may even behave badly, occasionally through embarrassment. Never allow yourself to be put in the position of colluding with pupils. If you think that your presence is creating difficulties, then it might be enough to leave the lesson and follow it up later. You should not intervene unless not to do so would pose a health and safety risk or seriously compromise the school's discipline and your own position. This is the worst-case scenario, but it could happen, so you need to have given it some thought.

Another issue is whether or not you participate in the lesson. Most people find it hard to be entirely passive observers, but if this is what you have agreed, then you should stick to it, unless the teacher asks you to join in. Whether you participate or not may depend on the focus. If you are in the lesson to observe a particular group of pupils, then it makes sense to sit and work with them. In a general observation it also makes sense to move around and talk to groups and individuals, if the style of lesson permits this. In the end, the best way to find out what pupils know, understand and can do is to talk to them about their work. This will give you a valuable insight into the effectiveness of the teaching. Remember though that if you do this, it limits what you will observe of the class as a whole and thus what you can feed back about the overall pattern of the lesson. Whatever you agree about participation, remember that you must stick to the agreement. When observing, you may think there is a serious problem and you will need to deal with this. We do not do anyone, least of all the teacher, any favours if we ignore this. However, schools have systems for dealing with competence and if you do find yourself in this situation you must make sure that you follow the correct procedures.

5 In the classroom: does it work?

The preparation is done, the ground rules are established, and you are about to embark on an observation. The first thing to recognise is that you will make mistakes. Observing is a skill which, like any other, can be learned and which improves with practice.

Knowing your own preferences

One of the hardest parts is leaving your own professional 'baggage' at the classroom door. The fundamental question is 'Does it work?' not 'Is this how I would teach?' You will have definite views on how things should be taught including the best resources to use, seating arrangements, the type of differentiation to use, the approach to take when introducing a new topic, etc. Remember that what works for you, with your level of experience, may not work as well for others. Be open-minded, prepared to accept that another approach may also work as well and that you too could learn from the observation.

Another common failing when observing is making overall judgements too early in a session. It is not easy to suspend judgement, but you do need to get a feel for what is happening and make factual notes initially. Many observers have found that they have made a note of something they thought was missing in the lesson, for example no use of ICT, only to find a few minutes later that the teacher has covered this as the lesson develops.

Entering the classroom

If this is a general observation, what are you actually going to do when you open the classroom door? To start with, try to create a relaxed atmosphere, smile and be friendly. Remember the normal courtesies. Don't forget that even if you are well known to the pupils, your presence will change the dynamics of the lesson. The teacher is also likely to be nervous, particularly if observation is not well established in the school. We all like to think that we are friendly and non-threatening but this may not be a teacher's perception when you come to observe, even if you normally have a very good working relationship.

An experienced teacher can be more nervous than an NQT or recently qualified teacher since the latter are used to being watched on teaching practice. The experienced teacher may be regarded by colleagues as a role model or may indeed be a mentor for an NQT, and therefore has a lot more to lose if the observer doesn't think it is a very good lesson. This can come as a surprise, particularly if you think the colleague is a confident and highly competent teacher. Stories of senior staff who forget what they are saying, react in an uncharacteristic manner to pupils and even drop piles of books are not unknown. So you really do need to think about how you are going to prepare and the sort of climate you want to create. The previous comment about needing to know where you will sit in the classroom may seem not worth mentioning let alone repeating. However, hesitating in the doorway is a very easy way to create unnecessary tension.

■ Observing the start

It is essential to arrive at the lesson on time. Not only is this good manners but you should not cause any disruption by coming in while the lesson is getting underway. Seeing how a lesson starts is very important. You can gauge a great deal about relationships, attitudes and teaching skills from the way in which the class arrives and is greeted, but be careful to suspend your judgement until you have seen more. As the lesson gets going you can start to make notes on what is happening, keeping in mind key factors. Make a note of the time when the introduction started and how long it lasted. Note down how links were made with previous work. If you can, use the actual words spoken. Look at the type of questions being used. Are general questions followed up with directed questions, for example:

- Who remembers how we finished off the last lesson?

- Peter, what happened to the copper when we heated it? What colour was the flame? What did the reaction between copper and heat produce?

- Samira, how was this different from what happened when we heated the other substances?

Note down how the pupils respond to question and answer sessions. If a general question is asked, what proportion of pupils want to answer and how many wait to be asked directly? Are pupils confident enough to risk making a mistake? How do others in the class react to this? How does the teacher use pupils' mistakes and misconceptions to move the work on? What sorts of question do pupils ask? Do they volunteer information? If the teacher is demonstrating or using the board, can all pupils see what is happening?

Did the teacher share the objectives with pupils? Listen for statements such as:

- By the end of the lesson you should all be able to explain why Shakespeare calls Romeo and Juliet 'star-crossed' lovers.

- Today we are carrying on with the work on techniques of shading in observational drawing.

- By the end of the lesson everyone should be able to identify at least three reasons why Britain went to war in 1914.

- By the end of this lesson you should all have completed your flowchart on the effect of enzymes on carbohydrates.

In some schools it is standard practice for teachers to write up the objectives on the board. Is reference made to this or is it assumed that because the aim is written up, all pupils will understand it? Is the aim written in language that most pupils understand?

▉ Pace and timing

Is there a smooth transition between activities so that pupils aren't given the chance to slide off-task? Are the instructions given clearly so that each individual (or group) knows exactly what to do, how long they have in which to do it, and can get started? Are all the resources which will be needed readily available and do the pupils know where to find them? What sort of pace is the teacher setting? Is there a sense of urgency? Listen for remarks such as:

- You have ten minutes to complete this section.

- By 10.15 each group should be ready to report back to the whole class.

If the class is working independently or in small groups, is the teacher circulating to challenge, encourage and keep different groups motivated and deal with issues as they arise? Is the teacher confident enough to adjust the lesson if it doesn't go quite according to plan? How does he or she manage the situation when the lesson gets diverted into an interesting discussion which is valuable, but not really planned? If the pupils haven't understood as much as the teacher thought, comments like these indicate a flexible approach:

- Let's go back over this.

- I think we need to do some more work on this before we start the new topic.

- It was obvious from the homework that most of you haven't really understood this properly. Let's have another look at it.

If a number of pupils are asking the same or similar questions, is the teacher able to use these as whole class teaching points? Or does he or she answer the same question several times with different pupils? If disaster strikes, and it can happen to anyone (perhaps the video doesn't work or the computers crash), what sort of back-up activity or coping strategy does the teacher have? A good teacher has the confidence to scrap a prepared lesson if it obviously isn't working and try something else, even when being observed. However, if this is happening too often, there may be an issue about the match of work to the needs of the class, or class management skills.

Using the planning

During the course of the session, look at the lesson planning. Teachers at different levels of experience are likely to need and use different levels of planning. The inexperienced teacher should have detailed planning which clearly identifies the learning objectives, all the activities, resources, differentiation, relationship with IEPs, EAL needs, use of support staff. An experienced teacher will probably have much less detailed notes, but you should still be able to see a relationship to a scheme of work in what is planned for a lesson. Can you identify learning objectives clearly?

Look at the match between the planning and the reality of the lesson. Has the teacher planned enough work to keep the pupils fully and profitably occupied for the whole lesson? Is there a clear structure, in most lessons, of introduction, development of the activity and review?

Is this matched by the actual structure of the lesson? Is the work differentiated, and if this is by outcome rather than task, does it allow for different levels of response? Is the supposedly open-ended task actually open-ended? If the worksheet has structured questions of increasing difficulty, is there actually enough time for the potentially higher attainers to reach these questions?

Is it evident from the planning that the lesson is building systematically on previous work? How is the teacher making sure that the pupils will make progress? Are there indications that the work is linked to a National Curriculum attainment target or an aspect of an exam syllabus? Do the plans include differentiation? Is there always enough work for pupils to do so that if there are problems with some pupils, others can, at the very least, get on with something productive? Is there scope in the planning for an evaluation, however brief, which goes beyond the 'went well' comment and enables the teacher to refine the planning for the next lesson or series of lessons? These are questions that lesson plans might prompt. Remember that what you are seeing are working plans that may be written many ways. You are looking at how effective the planning is in promoting good teaching, not whether you would plan in exactly the same way.

▮▮ Pupils' response

Talk to the pupils as much as possible (but always within the context of what you have agreed with the teacher). Ask them to tell you about their work. Useful questions include:

- What do you think you have learned in this lesson that you didn't know before?

- Do you think that you understand what you are doing better than you did before?

- What do you like best about this subject?

- How does this work fit in with what you have already done?

- Do you know what you are going to do next?

- How is your work marked?

- Do you get grades or marks? Do you know what these mean?

- How helpful are the comments?

- Do you set targets for yourselves?

When you are observing the pupils' reaction to the lesson, look at how they are behaving. Do they seem interested and engaged by the topic? Are they listening to the teacher and to each other? If working in groups, are they talking about the work (ignoring the occasional comment about what they did at the weekend, or what they intend to watch on television that night)? What sort of questions are they asking? Do they ask for help when they have tried hard for themselves but got stuck, or before they really need it? If the lesson is an investigation or a problem-solving activity, are they asking the 'What if' or 'What happens next' questions? Go back to a group after a few minutes and see what they have done.

▓ Observing the end of the lesson

At the end of the lesson, is there time for at least a brief review of what has been achieved? Again listen for phrases such as:

- Let's recap on what we have done today.

- Emma, tell me one thing you have learned about photosynthesis.

- Mohammed, what can you add to what Emma has said?

The teacher may also remind the pupils of what will come next, for example:

- Next lesson we will be using the tactical skills practised today to play a short game.

- Next lesson we will be using the video camera to record your presentations so that we can evaluate and work on them further.

If there isn't time for a review and this is indicated in the plan, is this because the lesson has been mis-timed? If so, what could the teacher do about it? Did the introduction last too long? Was he or she over-ambitious in what was prepared or did the class work more slowly than expected? Did the teacher have to spend too much time dealing with low-level disruption? If so, was this to do with the material or the teaching style, or is it something which needs discussing with the tutor or head of department to find out whether other staff are having problems with a class or a group?

Don't be rigid in your expectations of the lesson. A good lesson will not necessarily follow a prescribed pattern. Does the lesson which leaves pupils eagerly anticipating what they are going to do next really need a review?

Leaving the lesson

On leaving the lesson at the end of the observation, make sure that you thank the teacher. If your feedback is not taking place immediately after the lesson, and there are usually good reasons for this, check that you both know when and where it will take place. It is preferable to stay for the whole of the lesson, but if you have to leave part way through, make sure at the very least that you make eye contact, smile and indicate your thanks. In these circumstances, make a point of finding the teacher as soon as possible to say thank you and check that you both know when and where the feedback will be.

There are strong arguments in favour of some delay between observation and feedback to give both you and the teacher time to reflect on what you have seen. Feedback should, however, take place no longer than 24 hours after the observation. Any longer than this and the impact of the lesson is lost.

The learning environment

In any sort of observation, it is worth noting the condition of the room and how well it is arranged. Where there is scope to move furniture, is it arranged in such a way as to make the lesson run more smoothly and in a layout which is appropriate to the activity? Does the room reflect the subject being taught? Are the displays helpful in providing a rich environment? For example, in a mathematics room, does the display provide information about key mathematical vocabulary and concepts which pupils can use? In a food technology room, is there information about nutrition and healthy eating on display? Are the safety rules prominent in a laboratory or workshop? Does the teacher make any use of the display, by reference to it where appropriate or by asking pupils to examine artefacts or pictures? Is the display used to celebrate pupils' achievements? Are the displays well presented and up-to-date?

▇▇▇ Observing other aspects of the school's work

The pastoral system in a school is a key element in its success, as is the provision for special educational needs. Sessions with a tutor group, special needs, and EAL support, whether in class or withdrawal, can be observed as you would any other teaching activity and the same criteria apply. If joining a small group, be careful of the impact that another person may have. You will be more obvious than in a full lesson and may be more of a distraction.

▇▇▇ Interviews with parents and pupils

A year head, a SENCO, a pastoral deputy, or senior teacher is likely to spend a lot of time on individual casework, frequently interviewing pupils and their parents either to investigate a situation and establish both what has happened and what needs to be done, or to review progress. These meetings may normally never be observed. If, however, it is the usual routine to have another person present, then he or she can be asked in advance to give some feedback on the conduct of the interview. This can easily be done when discussing the outcome of the interview,

In this setting, if it is not the custom to have two people present for an interview, then the presence of another teacher could be seen as intimidating and will need careful handling. Parents and pupils must be asked if they have any objections to this and be given assurances about confidentiality. It may be helpful if the second teacher is someone known at least to the pupil, but this is not always an advantage. It is important that the observer is not someone to whom the pupil might feel hostile.

As an observer, you will be looking at the effectiveness of the interviewer in establishing a positive atmosphere where parents and pupil are confident that they will be dealt with fairly. Has the teacher prepared properly for the meeting and let the parents have all the relevant information in sufficient time? If an interpreter is needed, is it someone in whom the family will have confidence? Do the layout of the room and the seating arrangements help to establish the right sort of atmosphere? Are the types of question asked helping to establish what really happened or what the main issues are? Are there opportunities for the parents or the pupil to ask questions and put their point of view? If this is basically a disciplinary matter, are the pupil and parents getting a fair hearing? All these contribute to a successful meeting. How the teacher deals with possible conflict is also worth noting.

You can help the teacher to evaluate the success of the meeting and perhaps draw some general conclusions about techniques which are successful. The interviewer might be particularly good at putting people at their ease or summing up the decisions which have been made. You should be able to explain how this is achieved, for example the use of encouraging or constructive and positive comments; a friendly manner which is not patronising or condescending; the ability to focus on the issues and not the personality. The importance of body language can be over-stated but the amount of eye-contact and the degree of attention shown by the participants are things which may not be apparent to the interviewer either personally or in relation to the other people present.

It may also be helpful to analyse the reaction of parents, pupils and staff to criticism. If an interview has not gone particularly well then it should be possible to work out why. It may simply be that the parents or carers were still too angry and upset to be able to discuss the situation, or that there has been a real conflict of interpretation of events. Here an analysis of what was actually said could be helpful. If the parents did not understand the issue, did the teacher try to restate it in different ways? Was it suggested that a brief break to allow someone to calm down or get over being upset might be helpful? Did the teacher explain clearly what the next steps would be?

▓▓▓ Assembly

Another aspect of school life – the formal assembly, whether of the whole school, key stage, or year groups – is regularly observed but how often is it evaluated? Most schools now have a programme for assembly, and feedback would be useful, both in terms of the suitability of the themes and the impact on the pupils. Are the pupils generally listening and attentive? If involved in the assembly, have they been properly prepared and rehearsed so that they know what to do? How do the other pupils respond to what their friends and classmates are doing? Can the teacher create the right sort of atmosphere? Is the talk pitched at a level which the pupils can understand but at the same time makes them think and widens their horizons? Does the assembly help to teach the children how to behave on a formal occasion?

If the assembly is the setting for an act of collective worship, does this meet statutory requirements? Do pupils have opportunities for prayer or reflection? Over a period of time, are the acts of worship broadly Christian in character, unless of course the school has been allowed to modify its act of worship? Many schools frequently invite visitors to take assembly. Have they been briefed about what to expect? Is the visitor properly introduced so that the school is prepared for what will happen? How do pupils respond to the visitor?

Whatever the type of observation, be as factual and as detailed as possible in what you record. Don't rush to judgement and remember that what you record will form the basis of your feedback to the teacher.

6 Observation forms

Making notes is an essential part of observation and the teacher should be aware that this will happen and understand why. Don't be tempted to think that you will remember what happened. With the best will in the world, you won't be able to. As soon as you leave the room, other events and your own teaching will crowd in, and you will forget the detail.

All records of lessons should contain basic information, for example:

- class size;
- other adults present;
- type of lesson, e.g. whole class/group/individual work, mixed ability/set;
- length of time spent observing;
- the date;
- name/initials of teacher;
- name/initials of observer.

You will develop your own abbreviations when making notes, but remember that what you write forms the basis of post-observation discussion and, if possible, you want to avoid having to write up another record of the observation later on. This means that your abbreviations must be intelligible to others.

The key aim of the observation is to help the teacher to improve on his or her teaching by reflecting on what happened. So, when making notes, the more detail you can manage the better. Think about feeding back to the teacher, possibly 24 hours later, and what would be useful for this. Simply writing down statements such as:

- a reasonably good match with planning;
- satisfactory probing questions;
- brisk pace;
- good relationships.

may well be accurate judgements, but they won't be very helpful to you as discussion points. However, notes like the following give you more information and provide the starting point for discussing how the work can be better matched to the needs of all pupils or how the teacher can build on the good start to sustain the pace:

- 2/3rds took the 20 mins allowed, found task quite hard, but finished it. Too easy for 5 higher attainers who finished in 10 mins and too hard for the 3 SEN pupils who didn't finish.

- Q – 'How do you know whether this evidence is reliable?' followed with 'Look closely at the text and make a note in your books of two sentences which tell you who wrote the document and when it was written. What do these tell you about reliability?'

- All but a few completed the task unaided, SEN pupils succeeded when supported by SNA.

- Quick Q&A session set the class off at a brisk pace. Ps had to work hard to complete the task in the time allowed.

- T pleasant and polite to Ps, made expectations clear, voice well modulated, Ps relaxed but not familiar in their attitude.

- Technical vocab explained, Ps learnt key words, e.g. hegemony.

The format for the recording will vary depending on the type of observation. For a general observation, a sheet with a series of headings to match the prompt sheet you use for identifying the characteristics of good teaching would be suitable. Some observers may prefer simply to have a blank sheet of paper so that they can note down anything which strikes them as relevant or significant. This may occasionally be appropriate but it runs the risk of lacking direction. It is also harder to ensure consistency in the application of criteria if the observer is not prompted to consider certain aspects of teaching. This could lead to difficulties with staff who may feel that they are not being observed on the same basis as other staff. This is very important in relation to threshold applications. However, a well-designed form which includes space for additional comments need not constrain unduly. For a focused observation, you need to use an appropriate schedule which you may have to develop for the specific purpose. On this type of sheet, it is always helpful to leave space for additional comments.

To grade or not to grade?

To grade the observation or not is an important issue which is likely to be raised. You need to ask what use the grade will be and to whom. The very real danger of grading is that the 'mark' given for the lesson becomes more important than the comments. The teacher may become over-concerned about whether he or she has 'passed'. This can get in the way of constructive discussion as both teacher and observer can become hung up on what the grade means rather than how to improve the teaching.

If grading is used, then it is important to maintain a sense of perspective about it. A grade given for one lesson is not the definitive judgement on a teacher's work. A lesson is seldom wholly unsatisfactory and, equally, very few lessons cannot be improved at all. Most lessons are at least satisfactory which means that the teacher is competent and the pupils are making reasonable progress. In general, teachers do not regard a 'satisfactory' grade as satisfactory! Most 'satisfactory' lessons also have good features and more strengths than weaknesses, so an overall judgement of 'sound' or 'satisfactory' can be misleading.

 OFSTED forms

The OFSTED evidence form is essentially a blank sheet, which enables the observer to make a judgement on any aspect of the lesson being observed and to make clear links between teaching, learning, attainment and response (OFSTED *Handbook for Inspecting Secondary Schools*, January 2000). This allows a great deal of flexibility, but is probably best used by experienced observers because it assumes a detailed knowledge of the OFSTED criteria and does not include prompts. A teacher who does not do a great deal of observation is likely to be better served by a more structured format because it is easy to overlook key points unless prompted to do so.

 DfEE Performance Management forms

The DfEE *Model Performance Management Policy* (DfEE, June 2000, pp. 19–21) suggests summary forms that could be derived from information gained using a time log to record what happened in the lesson observed. The forms use the Performance Management headings (see also Chapter 3).

DfEE Performance Management Framework
Lesson Observation: Summative Assessment

Date: Teacher:

Lesson: Observer:

	Excellent	Good	Satisfactory	Development needed	N/A
1. The teacher plans effectively and sets clear objectives that are understood.	☐	☐	☐	☐	☐
2. The teacher shows good subject knowledge and understanding.	☐	☐	☐	☐	☐
3. The teaching methods used enable all pupils to learn effectively.	☐	☐	☐	☐	☐
4. Pupils are well managed and high standards of behaviour are insisted upon.	☐	☐	☐	☐	☐
5. Pupils' work is assessed thoroughly.	☐	☐	☐	☐	☐
6. Pupils achieve productive outcomes.	☐	☐	☐	☐	☐
7. The teacher makes effective use of time and resources.	☐	☐	☐	☐	☐
8. Homework is used effectively to reinforce and extend learning.	☐	☐	☐	☐	☐

Conclusions and feedback:

Strengths:

Areas for development:

Teacher's comments (optional):

DfEE Performance Management Framework
Lesson Observation: Time/Events Log
(If used, this should be completed during the lesson.)

Date: Teacher: Sheet No:

Lesson: Observer:

Time	Activity code	Description of activities in the classroom	Aspect

Suggested activity code

1 = Whole class interactive (teacher directed)   5 = Classroom management
2 = Whole class lecture   6 = Testing/assessment
3 = Individual work   7 = Transition between activities
4 = Collaborative work

▓▓ Creating suitable forms

Many schools find it helpful to devise their own format for recording observation and to give themselves flexibility. The way in which you might want to record a tightly focused observation is likely to be different from a general one.

▓▓ General observation

The first three forms that follow were designed for general observation. They could be used as part of a subject or departmental review.

- The form on page 50 could be used with the prompt list derived from the TTA standards or as a summary sheet for any observation. A completed version appears on page 51.

- The forms on pages 52–3 are derived from the OFSTED guidance on classroom observation.

- Some observers like to write a letter or report instead of giving the teacher a copy of the observation notes. The report must be structured, so that the main points are clear. Examples appear on pages 54 and 55.

▓▓ Focused or specific observation

Examples of forms designed for specific purposes follow on pages 56–61.

- The form used for the observation of NQTs follows the school's prompt list. It provides evidence for the summary. See pages 56–7.

- The form on page 58 shows how a school has customised a form for a specific purpose, in this case a departmental review, by adding prompts and an extra section to an OFSTED form.

- A timelog for a 60-minute lesson where time management was the focus appears on page 59.

- A grid for a lesson where the questioning technique is the main focus appears on page 60.

- See page 61 for a variation on the question log that enables the observer to feedback on pupil involvement.

OBSERVATION FORM

Teacher: Lesson:

Class: Date:

Subject: Number present:

Observer:

Context of the lesson:

Knowledge and understanding:

Planning:

Teaching and class management:

Monitoring, assessment and recording:

Other significant evidence/future development:

OBSERVATION FORM

Teacher: XY

Class: Y11

Subject: History

Observer: AB

Lesson: 1.30-2.30

Date: 2/8/01

Number present: 24/25

Context of the lesson: Content, NC attainment target(s) where relevant, GCSE final lessons on New Deal Class working in grps preparing presentation on pro and anti attitudes.
Resources: text books, notes, extracts from contemp. publications, extracts from interviews. Initial intro then Ps worked in grps with different source material to prepare presentation. Two lessons for preparation. Presentations in final lesson of the week.

Knowledge and understanding:
Secure – confident answers to Qs about personalities and issues.

Planning:
Learning objectives explained but mostly general e.g. Ps will understand attitudes better, no specific mention of the skills involved.
Clear structure: whole class intro, supported grp work, brief summary, approx time allowances.
Mixed grps teacher selected – different levels of work within the task for each group.

Teaching and class management:
Lively intro: Using Q&A, targeted so most Ps responded. Reminder of previous week's work and setting up task. 'What info will you need? Where will you find it?' Gd diagram built up on blackboard. Ps keen to respond. Intro longer than intended.
Task sheet gave clear guidance on grp organisation, available resources, use of library, use of IT, list of key points to be covered.
Move to grp work well managed, clear time targets: 'In 10 mins you should have decided who is doing what and by 2.15 each group should be able to report to the whole class on what they have done so far.'
Gd relationship with class – friendly but not familiar, consistent enforcement of rules, orderly classroom.
Ps settled well, asked Qs for guidance/clarification, one grp used CD-ROM for research, 1 sent 2 Ps to library.
No time for summing up – why was review needed, brief reminder about next lesson be enough?
Reading level of materials too difficult for 2 SEN statemented Ps.
Gd working atmosphere in the room – buzz of activity, noise within reasonable bounds.
Ps were able to find paper and book resources easily, IT more of a problem – limited access to computers and 2 grps wanted to use it.
Ps consolidating knowledge of New Deal, three grps using docs well – asking Qs about provenance and reliability, one grp confused until T picked it up.

Monitoring, assessment and recording
Initial Qs used well to check recall of info e.g 'What can you tell me from last week about attitudes to the New Deal?' Missed opportunity to probe further into how they would evaluate the different types of material e.g. What reliability tests would they use? Supportive work with grps, analysing what they were doing, making suggestions for improvement and additional resources they might consult. Suggestions made for further work at home, no formal homework set.

Other significant evidence/future development
Significant contribution to literacy for most Ps: drafting, higher order reading skills (NB: but not for SEN pupils). More access to IT needed.

ADDINGTON HIGH SCHOOL

**CLASSROOM OBSERVATION SCHEDULE – QUALITY OF TEACHING,
QUALITY OF LEARNING AND CLASSROOM MANAGEMENT**

Class   Subject: Teacher: Period: Date:

Quality of teaching	✓	Comments

1. Teacher gives clear communication of:
  • aims of lesson
  • tasks to achieve aims
  • homework		

2. Prompt and smooth transmission from one activity to the next		
3. Teacher actively monitors and supervises the progress of students		
4. Logical sequenced order of activities		
5. Teaching strategies match learning aims		
6. Evidence of differentiation		
7. Variety of teaching styles used		
8. A suitable pace is maintained in the lesson		
9. Students are inspired and challenged		
10. Time, support staff and learning resources, especially ICT, used effectively		
11. Work is assessed thoroughly		
12. Homework is used effectively		
13. Teacher shows good subject knowledge and understanding		

Targets:

Quality of learning (progress)		
1. Students understand aims of lesson		
2. Students are actively engaged on task		
3. Evidence of progress in Literacy, Numeracy, ICT		
4. Teacher intervenes with individuals/groups to develop learning		
5. Questioning is used to extend knowledge and understanding		
6. Students are able to summarise what has been learnt		
7. Groups are organised to maximise learning		
8. Students appreciate need for accuracy and good presentation		
9. Students sustain concentration, think and learn for themselves		
10. Students understand what they are doing, how well they have done and how they can improve		
Targets:		
Classroom management		
1. Clear orderly start to the lesson		
2. Resources are accessible and well used		
3. Teacher encourages progress through praise and reward		
4. Lesson comes to an orderly conclusion		
5. Teacher has positive relations with students		
6. Classroom is a learning environment		
7. Register is marked		
8. Poor behaviour is addressed appropriately		
Targets:		

OBSERVATION FORM

Teacher: AB

Class: Y7 mixed ability

Subject: German

Observer: CD

Lesson: Period 4

Date: 29/09/99

Number present: 24/25

Context of the lesson:
Class learning Gm for approx 3 wks. Using birthdays as stimulus for learning about the calendar.

Knowledge and understanding:
Gd pronunciation and accent, confident speaker, could answer all Qs.

Planning:
Clear structure to session, derived from SoW for KS3
Q&A session, followed by use of OHP to introduce new vocab and structured worksheets
(3 levels) notes for LSA to support statemented pupil.

Teaching and class management:
Gd rapport, manner pleasant and firm, speaks confidently, encouraging but not over-praising.
Clear but brief explanation of aims.
Routines: greeting class, taking register in Gm, giving out resources worked well.
Collection of hwk took too long (5 mins), 2 Ps had to explain why they hadn't done it, allowed
some to get noisy, T had to take time to re-establish quiet.
Ps seem to be enjoying lesson, respond eagerly to Q&A on vocab learnt in previous lesson.
Balance Gm and En about right, En used to clarify tasks, at least two thirds of lesson in Gm.
Clear instructions, class expected to be quiet and listen carefully.
Most Ps quickly learn how to ask partners about birthdays.
T uses the activity well to reinforce knowledge of numbers and months.
Display had days, months, and numbers easily visible – being used by T and Ps.
The follow-up worksheets at different levels of difficulty enabled the pupils to work at a suitable
level. The LSA supporting the statemented pupil had been well briefed, giving good support once
Ps were working independently.
Timing worked, Ps given 15 mins to complete wksheets, given 5 min reminder.
All but 2 Ps completed wk, had to concentrate hard to finish.
Wk pitched at the right level of difficulty for class. Discussion with Ps; T's quick recap
showed Ps had good understanding of vocab learnt – good progress.

Monitoring, assessment and recording
Q&A at start and finish used to test K&U targeted well.
Brief notes made at end of lesson. Brief discussion with LSA while class were busy.
Hwk collected in.

Other significant evidence/future development
No ICT used. NB: planning shows use at other times. Write the aims on the whiteboard for
pupils to refer to? Breaking 'Geburtstag' down into two part, explaining each part might
have helped some Ps to grasp the vocab more quickly. Making links with similar patterns
in Eng is worth considering.

Teacher: AB   Class/subject: 7X German
Observer: CD (senior manager   Date/time: 29th Sept 1999 Period 4
                    attached to dept.)
Copy to: EF (HoD)

I enjoyed visiting your Y7 German lesson yesterday and thank you for the lesson plan. It was very helpful in putting the lesson into context. I thought that the work you were doing was well planned and pitched at the right level of difficulty for the class who had been learning German for only about three weeks. You have established a good rapport with the class and your manner with them is pleasant and firm. You speak to them confidently and are encouraging without over-praising. The routines of greeting the class, taking the register in German and giving out resources are well understood.

The pupils appear to be enjoying what they are doing and they respond eagerly to the question and answer sessions. Question and answer sessions at the start and finish were both well structured to enable you to test knowledge and understanding and monitor progress. The balance of use of German and English is about right for the class. Your own accent and pronunciation are good.

You clearly expect the pupils to be quiet and listen carefully to instructions. The work on days, dates and birthdays was well structured and most pupils quickly learnt how to ask their partners when their birthdays were. You used the activity well to reinforce their knowledge of numbers and months. The use of the display was effective in providing some basic vocabulary and information. The follow-up worksheets at different levels of difficulty enabled the pupils to work at a suitable level. The LSA supporting the statemented pupil had been well briefed and was able to give good support once the pupils were working independently and give you some helpful feedback during the lesson. You judged the time well and set suitable time targets. Almost all the pupils had to work hard to complete the work. My own conversations with them as well as your re-cap at the end of the lesson showed that they had understood the work and made good progress.

Overall the lesson was good and successfully matched your planning, but there were one or two areas, which need some further consideration.

1) The explanation of the aims at the start of lesson was clear, but a bit brief. You might consider writing the aims on the whiteboard, so that the pupils can refer to them, as they did to the vocabulary on display.

2) Some of the pupils were a little slow to grasp the vocabulary and it might have been easier to break 'Geburtstag' down into two parts, e.g. 'geburt' and 'tag' and explain what each part meant. Making links with similar patterns in English is worth considering.

3) Collecting in homework took longer than it need have done. (Could you have dealt more briskly with the two pupils who had not done their homework or asked them to wait at the end of the lesson?). This allowed a few of the class to become rather restless and noisy so that you had to work quite hard to re-establish quiet.

I look forward to being able to observe your teaching again at some time in the future, but in the meantime keep up the good work.

ADDINGTON HIGH SCHOOL
NQT LESSON OBSERVATION

Name: Faculty: Date:

Period: Room: Group:

Subject:

Topic:

Planning and preparation:

Subject expertise:

Classroom management:

Management of learning activities, including differentiation:

Pupil learning, including differentiation:

Assessment skills, record keeping:

Classroom presence:

Observation and evaluation:

Additional comments:

Newly qualified teacher . . . .

Faculty staff . . . .

Faculty head . . . .

Staff development co-ordinator . . . .

ADDINGTON HIGH SCHOOL
NQT SUMMARY OF OBSERVATION

Classroom Observation:

Teacher: . . . .   Date: . . . .

Lesson observed: . . . .   Year: . . . .

Number of pupils: . . . .   Group: . . . .

Context of lesson observation:

Conclusions:

Agreed targets:

Signed . . . .

ROSEBERY INTERNAL REVIEW LESSON OBSERVATION FORM

Context of the observation: **Teacher's name:**

Content
Activities
Organisation
Adults' roles

Teaching:

Enthusiasm
Knowledge
Expectations/challenge
Planning
Methods/grouping
Discipline
Use of time
Assessment
Homework
SEN/EO

☐

Grade

Response:

Attitudes
Behaviour
Relationships
Learning skills
Participation

☐

Grade

Progress:

New knowledge
Consolidation
High attainers
Low attainers
SEN/EO

☐

Grade

School policies:

Expectation for teaching at Rosebery
Teaching and learning policy
Behaviour policy
Assessment policy
Departmental policy

☐

Grade

Other significant evidence (e.g. language skills, numeracy, SMSC, staffing, accommodation, resources):

Use grades 0 or 1–7:
0 = insufficient evidence   1 = excellent   2 = very good/well above average
3 = above average   4 = satisfactory/about average   5 = below average
6 = poor/well below average   7 = very poor

Class: 1OCD | **No. present: B** 14 **G** 12   **Abs** O
Subject/context: English | **Teacher:** CD   **Observer:** AB
Special features: SNA present to | **Date:** Tues 27/3   **Time:** Period 2
    work with 2 statemented pupils |

Brief description of lesson content: GCSE set text – character analysis

Time	Activity	Comments
Lesson start 10.00	Register taken. Homework collected.	School policy followed on registers and hwk. Contact bks used to let parents know about missing hwk. Slow start to lesson but friendly atmosphere. Latecomer dealt with promptly.
10.10	Whole class Q&A re-cap on previous lesson.	Picks up after slow start. Brisk Q&A, targeting questions to individuals – varying degrees of difficulty, about 2/3rds involved.
10.15	Wksheets given out, class working in small groups analysing roles and motivation of the key characters. Work to be collated into booklet for whole class.	Routines well established, clear time frame, grps have 30 mins before reporting back. SNA briefed before the lesson to support SEN group, 2 levels of wksheets giving prompts for the Ps.
10.30	Teacher circulates asking questions and supporting group work.	Mostly quiet talking about the work, but 3 groups need reminding of need to concentrate.
10.40	As above, teacher tells class when they have 5 mins left.	Most groups still working well – 2 groups of boys not working unless teacher or SNA works with them. Language of wksheet too difficult?
10.45	4 pairs allowed 2 mins each to report back.	Not enough time allowed for all to report back – more time promised in next lesson.
11.00 Lesson finish	Quiet finish to lesson. Reminder about need to bring work to next lesson.	School routine for dismissal followed. No real re-cap of lesson content – not enough time.

Other comments, e.g. resources, IT, SEN support, EAL

IT available, but not used this lesson – 1 grp asks to use next lesson to wp their presentation.
SNA makes brief records of what Ps have achieved.
Ps all have their own copy of the text.
Third in a sequence of 6 lessons.
Teacher made evaluative notes of progress.
Reminders given about theatre visit.

Class: 9X	**No. present: B** 14	**G** 12 **Abs** 2
Subject/Context: KS3 Science	**Teacher:** AB	**Observer:** CD
mixed ability group	**Date:** 3/6/01	**Time:** Period 3
Special features: SNA present to work		
with 2 statemented pupils		

Brief description of lesson content:
Reactivity – second lesson in a series of four. Previous lesson on reactions with water; this lesson is on the reaction with acid, focus on potassium and sodium. AT1 and AT3

Question types	Questions directed to:		
	Whole class	**Individual boy**	**Individual girl**
Closed	X X	X	X
Open	X X	X X X	X X
Probing/ Follow up	X X	X X X X	X
Multiple	X	X X	
Leading	X X	X X X	X

Other comments/relevant points (e.g. ICT, resources, SEN support):
Questions worked well in developing technical vocab.
Boys targeted particularly – school policy?
SNA had lesson plan, made notes of work of her group to feedback,
SEN pupils managed practical with support.
ICT available, not part of this lesson plan, other plans show use.
Most of class (approx 3/4) had remembered main points of previous week's work.
Good relationship with class.
Good response to Q&A at start and finish, teacher picked up on mistakes, e.g. lack of precision in the description of the reaction of potassium, and used them. Good transition to practical work – no time wasted because resources ready.
Good buzz of activity – pupils asking 'What happens next?' questions.

PLAN OF CLASSROOM

✓ F F ✓✓	✓✓ ✓✓	✓✓	✓	✓ ✓ ✓
		✓	✓A	

✓ ✓	✓✓	✓	
	X✓	AF	A

X ✓	✓ F ✓✓	✓✓	✓ F ✓
			✓

A F X AX	✓	✓✓	✓✓	✓✓
	A A	✓✓	A A A X	

```
TEACHER'S
DESK
```

Whole group 卌 卌 卌
F   **follow-up question**
X   **negative feedback**
A   **teacher asked pupil**
✓   **volunteered response**

Other comments:
– Working in pairs after whole-class introduction on climate and weather, comparing UK and different areas of France.
– 1 hr lesson very long to sustain concentration. Despite several different activities, 4 pupils got restless, hence the negative feedback.
– P's oral knowledge better than reading skills; several pairs couldn't read vocab on the blackboard or in textbook.

Class: 8X   **Subject:** French middle set   **Time:** 2.30–3.30
Teacher: AB   **Observer:** EF   **Date:** 1/12/00

7 Feedback and follow-up

Feedback or debriefing is an integral part of the observation. This is where you can be of real assistance to the teacher in helping him or her to improve teaching. You can use the evidence of the observation to discuss strengths and points for development. When you have observed a teacher more than once, you can use comparative information and have an even more well-informed discussion.

You and the teacher must agree an appropriate time and place and ensure that you will be able to meet without interruption. Make sure that the place where you meet will help, not hinder, the discussion. The teacher's own classroom is often a good place to meet because, amongst other things, it enables you to refer to displays or look at books or resources. Face to face across your desk in your office or that of a senior member of staff is not usually helpful, particularly if you have some difficult messages to convey.

Allow enough time for feedback, but do not assume that it will take hours. Fifteen minutes or so should be long enough for the average lesson, though you might need longer with an inexperienced teacher. If you need more than this, then it suggests serious problems which may need different handling. Your approach and body language will convey messages. Make sure they are the right ones. It is very off-putting for the teacher if you create the impression that the feedback is being fitted into a very busy schedule and that you want to get it over with as quickly as possible. Don't take telephone calls, however important someone else thinks they are. Think about how you would like to receive feedback and be prepared to listen as well as talk.

Timing

The feedback should be soon after the end of the observation. Immediate feedback is often perceived as helpful because teachers are keen to know what you think about the lesson. However, comment can be difficult at this stage, particularly if it has to be rushed because neither of you has much time. Less experienced observers are likely to need time to think about what they have observed and pick out the salient points. A brief conversation can be useful, particularly if you have points which you wish to clarify. As you become more experienced in observing you will find it easier to give more immediate feedback, but always make sure that you have enough time.

There are arguments for not feeding back immediately but you do, however, need to discuss the lesson while it is still reasonably fresh in both your minds. Even with notes, it is easy to lose track of key points; aim to meet within 24 hours of the observation. Prepare carefully for the feedback by identifying the key points which you wish to cover. Focus as much as possible on the learning and the pupils' response, and use these as the means of introducing discussion about teaching. Make sure that you have identified the strengths and areas for improvement clearly and that you have the evidence to justify what you want to say.

In the vast majority of lessons, the strengths should significantly outweigh the weaknesses. This does not mean that there is nothing to feed back. In general, teachers do not receive anything like enough praise and appreciation for what they do. They are likely to respond well to feedback which is very clear about their strengths, many of which they may have taken for granted. Teachers also need to know what is working well and how they can use the most successful techniques to help the weaker areas. It is not uncommon, for example, to see good introductions which interest and motivate the class but do not produce written work of the same quality. An articulate and enthusiastic teacher may manage a discussion skilfully, using good visual stimuli and probing questions, and thus enable the pupils to show a good depth of knowledge. The problem could be with the structure of the task or resulting worksheet.

The feedback should help the teacher to see how the oral techniques which ensure good learning can be used to improve the quality of the written work. For example, questions could be structured with an incline of difficulty which mirrors the structure of the probing oral questions. The teacher may be good at explaining difficult concepts and vocabulary orally but not have given enough thought to doing this in a worksheet. He or she might be able to make more use of the expertise of the special needs or EAL staff. Pupils are used to very high quality presentation in commercially produced publications and so may be less tolerant of old worksheets or poor drawings or illustrations.

At the start of the feedback, give the teacher time to talk about his or her perceptions of the lesson. For a variety of reasons, the teacher may take a different view of the lesson from yours. Whether you agree or disagree, the teacher's views must be considered and are usually a good starting point. Try to ask questions which prompt further reflection, for example:

- What did you think of the lesson? How happy were you with how it went?

- How much did you achieve of what you expected to?

- What do you think worked best and why?

- How typical was this lesson with this class/group?

- What might you do differently the next time?

Open questions enable you to start a constructive discussion in which you can contribute your views and make sure important points are fully covered. If you are not clear about an aspect of the lesson, ask the teacher to explain why he or she took that course of action. Don't say this in such a way that the teacher assumes you are being negative. Make it clear that you are genuinely seeking information and clarification. Tone of voice is important. 'Why did you do that?' can be an intimidating or reassuring question.

If the teacher finds it difficult to analyse the lesson, be prepared to introduce your own analysis. Don't allow an awkward silence to develop as this could imply disapproval. Start your own comments with something positive. Use specific examples, such as:

- I thought your questioning at the beginning was effective because the questions were challenging and you matched them to the range of attainment in the class. I liked the way you made sure most pupils had a chance to join in.

- You explained the task very clearly and the class had no difficulty settling down to work. This made it easier for you to help the special needs pupils.

Move the discussion quickly on to how to use the good practice to support areas where the teacher may not be as strong. If the lesson is well structured but the pace is not sustained and not enough work is completed, your observation may help the teacher to see whether he or she has simply been a little over-ambitious in this lesson or whether the teacher is letting the pupils to set the pace. It could, however, be that there is a problem over time management or pupils' understanding of previous work.

It can be helpful to ask the teacher to bring samples of work to the feedback so that you can look at these together and compare the quality of work in class with what you have learned from reviewing planning or scrutinising pupils' books. This can be useful to teachers who may not have that opportunity if this is not part of normal routine.

▄▄ Dealing with difficulties

If you are concerned about what you have seen and have significant criticisms, you must find a way of making them. Most teachers know when a lesson hasn't gone well and if you fudge this aspect of the feedback, it undermines the teacher's confidence in your judgement. Similarly, we all know that what we do can almost always be improved upon. Over-praising the lesson which is satisfactory but not outstanding, or ignoring difficult issues, is neither credible nor helpful. On the other hand, a 'nitpicking' approach is not helpful either. It is better to leave the teacher with three or four key points which will really make a difference, rather than a long list of minor issues which may leave him or her feeling demoralised.

You must be honest when feeding back, but this does not mean being brutal. If a lesson hasn't gone very well, the teacher is likely to need support and time to talk through what has happened. You should, after a little while, be able to steer the conversation into more positive channels and begin to rebuild the teacher's confidence. It doesn't help if you start by telling him or her all the faults.

Concentrate on issues which will really make a difference and make sure you focus on the quality of teaching rather than the teacher's personality. An unsatisfactory lesson should lead to constructive professional dialogue, not personal criticism. You are there to help the teacher improve teaching. Make comments with specific reference to what you have seen, for example:

- You have said that you were disappointed in how much was done. Is this because the pace of the lesson was rather slow or hadn't they understood as much as you had expected from the previous work?

- Perhaps you didn't get as far as you had hoped because the pupils didn't know how much time they had to complete the work and they, rather than you, were setting the pace.

- The comprehension task was too easy for about half the class and they finished quickly, and I think this was why there were some behaviour problems. Could we look at how you might provide something more challenging for this group so that they don't have the opportunity to misbehave? Perhaps some extended writing or a piece of individual research? Would it help if you made it clear that they should always have their current reading book with them?

■ Giving advice

Be constructive in your feedback and aim to help the teacher to identify strategies which could improve the lesson. Don't be afraid to give the benefit of your experience, though it is usually counter-productive to say, 'This is what you must do.' As a more experienced teacher you should be able to suggest a range of options and discuss what might be most suitable. What works well for you may not be appropriate, and this could leave the teacher feeling frustrated and inadequate.

Make practical suggestions about what the teacher can do to consolidate or improve his or her general teaching skills. For example, pace is often an issue and the teacher might be concerned that not enough is finished in lessons. One possible way of dealing with this is to discuss with the teacher why it is important for the pupils to know what they have to do and how much time they have. Introducing the use of time targets to help keep pupils on task, together with regular reminders – for example, 'You have 10 minutes left' or 'Everyone should be doing Question 4 by now' – could be sufficient to resolve the problem.

The underlying issue could, though, be one of expectations or lesson planning. Your discussion could help the teacher to consider how much more the pupils are capable of doing. If the planning is not rigorous enough, discuss how you can focus more on learning objectives and setting short-term targets. Or you might look together at how the baseline information about the class could be used in the planning. Is the teacher underestimating what the pupils already know? Has the teacher looked at the exam results in comparative terms? If pupils are regularly doing better in other subjects or in other teaching groups in the same subject, what might the teacher learn from this?

If there are discipline problems, as a starting point, discuss ways of ensuring that those pupils who want to work can do so. You can help the teacher to see how perhaps a different structure to the lesson or seating arrangement could help deal with problems. Your feedback should help the teacher to understand the inter-relationship of different aspects of teaching.

With a teacher whom you are observing because of a specific issue of competence, you need to be very precise in your feedback as your evidence could form part of a disciplinary hearing. For example, if you are observing because there are concerns about the quality of planning, you should make sure that you are specific in your feedback about the effectiveness of the match between the planning and the quality of the lesson.

Feeding back to newly qualified or beginning teachers follows the same principles as for other teachers. A few key points are more useful than a long list of relatively minor issues. However, with an NQT you should be giving specific guidance.

The feedback should also identify what support will be available, whether this is a note to the professional development co-ordinator asking for help to find a suitable course, or the organisation of some observation of colleagues, or fixing the date of a meeting to look at planning or moderation of work. Setting targets with a teacher without identifying how help and support will be available is likely to be setting up failure.

Dealing with disagreement

There is always the possibility in giving feedback that the teacher may disagree with your evaluation of the lesson. This possibility is one reason why you must be quite certain that your observation record is accurate and factual. The observation record must provide the evidence you need to support your judgements. The observation record must also relate to objective criteria, not subjective opinion. Remember always that the discussion you have with the teacher should focus on the teaching and not on the person. Obviously, during the session you should try to resolve any differences of opinion. Ultimately, however, if you cannot reconcile the difference, the teacher has to have the right to ask for another observation or refer the matter to someone else. The school should have clear procedures for this situation in its observation policy.

Keeping a record

In the course of feeding back to the teacher, it is helpful to make notes of points that have been raised, so that both you and the teacher can have a copy, not just of the observation form, but of any points for action and follow-up. These notes can be done on a separate form or on the back of the observation form if this is possible. When you have finished the observation and feedback, it is a good idea to make a note of any future review/observation dates, give a copy of the record to the teacher, file the relevant information and destroy any unnecessary paperwork.

Avoiding mixed messages

If more than one person observes a teacher, as can be the case with an NQT or a beginning teacher, it is important to iron out any possible mixed messages in the feedback. That is not to say that the observers will not see lessons of different quality. Few teachers are uniformly excellent or uniformly poor. Most of us will have very good, good, and satisfactory lessons, and sometimes all in one day. The timing, the particular class, one's confidence in the material, can all have a profound effect on the success of a lesson. However, if there are significant differences of opinion then these must be discussed. This is particularly important in the case of NQTs where a poor observation on record could jeopardise the successful completion of the induction year. If this is likely to be the case then further observation is essential.

It could also happen, however, that during a routine sampling of lessons a senior manager takes a different view from a head of department. If the senior manager line-manages the department, he or she should know in any case what the situation is with regard to staff in the department. If a head of department has concerns, these should probably have been shared and the senior manager made aware of any targets set before undertaking the observation. It could easily undermine a head of department's authority, or a teacher's confidence, if a senior manager gives another message or wants different targets. Prior discussion can easily avoid this.

It may be more difficult to ensure that this does not happen if the senior manager is doing a general school survey or a tracking exercise. He or she may not line-manage the department and may therefore not have the same degree of knowledge of its work. Even in these circumstances, in a small school it is unlikely to be much of a problem and in a larger school could be dealt with by a note which outlines the programme and asks if there is anything which would be helpful for the observer to know. Information which might be confidential should be shared on a strictly 'need to know' basis.

8 Training for observation: methods and approaches

Training for observation is an important issue. Training is not always considered early enough when implementing a new observation policy, but it can be vital to its success. For example, mentors need to be confident that they have the skills to identify the key points which will really make a difference to the NQT or the beginning teacher's ability to control a class and teach the subject. For any observers, some work on the basic skills will help them to observe, confident that they understand the purpose of what they are doing and have at least identified the skills involved.

A teacher taking on responsibility for mentoring for the first time is likely to benefit from training. The judgements made on an NQT could have a significant effect on that teacher's career. Performance in the classroom is the single most significant aspect of the induction year and the mentor needs to be confident that his or her judgements on the quality of teaching will stand up to scrutiny. Even experienced teachers who are beginning to observe as part of a wider management responsibility may well benefit from some additional or 'top-up' training. We are not always aware of our own professional preconceptions or of the extent to which these may colour our view of the lessons we watch. At the very least, training should make us aware of these.

Training techniques

Training can use a number of techniques, but video, discussion of the elements of good teaching, and paired observation are the most common. Watching a video, whether professionally produced or videos of lessons in the school, is an effective way of introducing the topic. It is a useful technique, in the first instance, to ask the observers simply to make notes on what they see and not to make any judgements. Doing this for the first time shows teachers how hard it is not to rush to judgement. Asking the audience what they have noticed tends to produce judgements very quickly and often negative ones at that. This should be used as a salutary lesson. Inexperienced observers are particularly prone to do this. They are also more likely to be significantly critical. In a training session, a subject specialist in a mixed group also has a tendency to be critical.

Sharing what we have observed is a good way of revealing our professional 'baggage'. One observer might particularly notice the use of language in the classroom, another might be more interested in classroom organisation or the maintenance of good discipline. On one occasion, observers in a group watching a video disagreed about how many adults were present in the room because they were unconsciously focusing on different aspects. One was more interested in the work of the adults, the other in the work of a group of children. Another observer was struck by the fact that the standard of school uniform varied to a point which would not have been acceptable in his school. Another found the use of rather colloquial language disconcerting as he thought the teacher should be more formal in her approach to the teaching of a particular skill. Variations like these in what is observed provide points for useful discussion.

Whether using video or not, a discussion on common features one might expect to see, or how well the school's agreed policies are being implemented, should help all staff. However, the discussion of a group of specialists is likely to be rather different in that there will be a greater depth of subject knowledge and hence of analysis. For example, there are likely to be legitimate professional differences of opinion on the best approach to teaching a class about the digestive system, or Shakespeare's sonnets, or the significance of propaganda in wartime. A group of specialists might want to tease these out.

Paired observation

Paired observation is another effective method of training. Here two people watch the same lesson and compare notes about what they have seen and discuss the lesson with the teacher being observed. This obviously requires the agreement of another teacher who is willing to be observed in this way. However, in many schools teachers are very used to the presence of other adults, whether learning support assistants or EAL teachers, so they are not particularly disconcerted by two observers.

The observers must agree beforehand on the type of observation and what they will be expected to record, using an agreed format. They will not necessarily be in complete agreement over the quality of the lesson – teaching is not after all an exact science, but if they disagree wildly this needs considerable discussion and may indicate a subject problem. In any case, a three-way discussion with the teacher is important. He or she will have a view about the success of the lesson and this needs to be taken into account. The two observers must, however, be very careful not to become a joint 'inquisition' and leave the teacher feeling doubly demoralised. The usual rules about constructive feedback apply. The discussion in these small groups could then be extended so that the 'trio' can share experiences with other 'trios' and share helpful information about what has worked well as well as what to avoid.

Organising the training

The training sessions can be organised in a number of ways but these too need careful preparation and a clear understanding of purpose. Are your objectives clear? Is the day intended to introduce all staff to the principles of observation? Is it primarily for staff who are or will be observing other colleagues? Is it a refresher course where observation is well established but an update is needed because of a new national development? It could be that a number of new staff have not been trained. All these are possible reasons but appropriate training in one situation may not be appropriate in another.

A whole day given to training for all staff should probably include all the following elements:

- observing;
- recording;
- feedback with opportunity for discussion;
- role-play.

It would be desirable to use video, or it might even be possible to set up some demonstration lessons. Such a day could possibly also be linked to working on a whole-school policy or code of practice, if the school does not already have one. A series of 'twilight' sessions, focusing on the different aspects, is an alternative approach which perhaps enables more in-depth discussion of specific subjects. If paired observation is part of the training this must obviously be organised on a normal working day, but the outcomes could form a useful stimulus for discussion with a larger group. The paired observation would therefore need to precede the training day or twilight session.

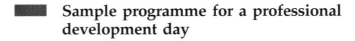 ## Sample programme for a professional development day

A programme for a day might look like this:

Programme for Professional Development Day
Classroom Observation

9.15	Coffee and introductions
9.30	Plenary session
	Why observe?
	General principles of observation
	Use of video extracts to highlight key points
10.30	Coffee
11.00	Extended video and group discussion
12.00	Plenary with questions from groups
12.30	Lunch
13.30	Work in groups on feeding back from observation notes
14.45	Plenary discussion and feedback from groups to provide headlines for a school policy

---

Sample programme for training in classroom observation

A programme for top-up training for new observers using paired observation might look like this:

Programme for Training in Classroom Observation
Week 1
16.00 to 17.30
Input from trainer/senior manager outlining the principles of observation and the criteria to be used.
Trios arrange pairings, agree observation times and focus.

Weeks 2 and 3
Observation and feedback at mutually agreed times.

Week 4
16.00 to 17.30
Trainer leads structured discussion on the process; trios invited to contribute and to raise questions.

Practical arrangements

The practical arrangements for training sessions need to be considered carefully. Training can all too easily fail if the day or session does not run smoothly. If the lead trainer is external to the school, has he or she been fully involved in planning the sessions and fully briefed about any significant issues? If you are using video, is it possible to have more than one copy so that staff can watch it in smaller groups? If not, is the screen big enough for all staff to see clearly? If not, where can you borrow one? For group discussion, have you briefed the group leaders properly? Have you allowed enough time in the programme for movement between sessions? Are the domestic arrangements well in hand?

 # Conclusion

Whatever approaches are used for training, the participants need to be aware that the training cannot deal with every possible circumstance and will not provide all the answers. As with teaching, the skills of observation develop with practice. Training needs to be followed up with real observation. The sooner you can get started the better, so that the teaching staff and the whole school can begin to benefit.

9 The role of governors in observing teachers

Most governors take their duties seriously, are genuinely interested in the school and want to support it. Many have become governors because it arises naturally out of their involvement as parents, others out of a sense of civic duty. Governors have an important role in the strategic management of schools and a number of statutory functions. The latter include ensuring that the National Curriculum is being taught, the delegated budget is being properly used, and the school has a performance management policy. Governors set targets for the headteacher and agree the salaries of the headteacher and deputies. They are involved in the appointment of staff, both teaching and non-teaching. They will discuss and approve a school development plan, the annual budget and, every so often, the OFSTED Action Plan.

Many governors are willing to be linked with a department or year group and will take interest in its work. They visit teachers, looking at samples of work to get an idea of what pupils are expected to know, understand and be able to do. Many participate in curriculum committees and read policy statements, though all the time expecting clear guidance on such matters from the professionals. Similarly, they expect from senior managers clear guidance on the reasons why they should be observing teachers and what they can expect to learn from the observation. Some feel that it is not the role of a governor to tell a teacher how to teach, or to judge on competence. This view highlights a misconception of the role of governors when observing. They are there to find out how the school works and what the pupils experience. Observation enables them to understand the significance of what they are discussing and should help them to make better informed decisions. Their comments may help teachers to understand more about what it is like to be a pupil in the school. Govenors bring their own experience and skills. Their different perspectives can be immensely valuable. They are not there to suggest how a teacher might improve his or her teaching.

Even the most experienced governors can feel ill-equipped to observe and reluctant to undertake it as part of their monitoring of the school's work. This is understandable, but somewhat paradoxical as most people recognise a good teacher when they see one. Even if lay observers cannot always explain why, their description of what is happening, followed up by a discussion with the teacher or head-teacher, can help to develop their understanding. The senior managers should be able to demonstrate to governors the benefits that will accrue from more detailed knowledge and understanding of the content of the curriculum, teaching methods, and resource needs.

The experience of OFSTED lay inspectors is encouraging in this context. Their role, once understood, is seldom resented. They want to understand why things are done in a particular way. They also recognise that it is not their job to give professional advice in the way that a teacher observing another teacher would be expected to do. The majority of them are shrewd observers who ask pertinent questions. These may well challenge the professionals to explain what they are doing in language which a lay person, whether parent or governor, can understand, and teachers should be capable of doing this. As a profession, teachers have not been good at explaining in plain English what they are trying to achieve. This has led to a wide range of misconceptions and misunderstandings, and often, when questioned, a defensive attitude on the part of the teachers. The need to explain in simple, but not patronising, terms has begun to break this down. Regular observation by governors should help to take it further.

If observation by governors is to become part of the routine work of the school, then the climate of trust is even more important than it is with teachers observing each other. It is sensible for governors and staff to have met, perhaps informally. A group of staff and governors might work together on a code of practice so that both understand why governors are observing and what the ground rules are. It is likely to be very similar to the code agreed with teachers.

Governors need to be well briefed so that they understand what they will be seeing. The teacher cannot assume that the governor will be familiar with school policies and the detail of schemes of work. Governors should be prepared to do some 'homework' before visiting. Background reading would be helpful but governors, like teachers, are pressed for time. A short briefing paper from each department (preferably no more than one to two sides of A4) which forms part of a school file might be more appropriate. This could highlight recent developments as well as briefing the governors about examination courses, results, staffing and resources. The senior management team should also consider providing governors with a brief update on progress on whole-school issues, if this does not form part of the regular reports to governors' meetings. As with teacher observers, governors should be pleasant and polite in classrooms, remembering that they are visitors in someone else's working area. Governors should try to have a brief word with the teacher at the end of the lesson to say thank you and, if time permits, to ask any questions.

Some thought needs to be given to the classes a governor might visit. It is not uncommon for parent governors to find themselves observing in classes where their children are pupils. Some will prefer not to be in the same classroom, others may have no concerns. Their feelings should be respected as the governors are likely to have a shrewd idea of how their presence will affect their sons or daughters!

Many governing bodies have a programme of visits during the school day as part of their routine monitoring. This could be as duty governors for a month or half a term. The governors attached to a specific subject or year group may be expected to visit for the equivalent of a day in a school year. The link governors for numeracy, literacy and special educational needs may also want to visit regularly. These visits are all likely to include spending time in classes as well as discussion with the headteacher, teachers and pupils. The governors taking part are usually expected to write a brief report for the next governors' meeting or appropriate committee. When visits involve classroom observation, the governors should be careful to write about learning and classes, not individual teachers.

Most observations will go smoothly but it is very important that the governors know how to deal with a potentially difficult situation. In the vast majority of cases, it would make sense to leave the lesson and seek advice. Often a short session with the headteacher or the head of department will already have been arranged and this, not the end of the lesson, is the time to raise concerns. Only if the governor feels that the pupils' safety is at risk should he or she intervene.

■ Sample school policy and code of conduct for observation

As part of its responsibilities, the governing body would expect to be consulted on and approve the school policy and code of conduct for observation. This will help governors to understand in greater depth the reasons why the school is instituting a programme of observation and their own role in it. The policy would, of course, need to be kept under review to ensure that it meets the school's needs and complies with any statutory requirements. See pages 77–9 for a sample policy and code of conduct.

CLASSROOM OBSERVATION POLICY

Observation should be part of normal routine in each department and year group and for the senior management team. It should be an integral part of staff development and school improvement and linked closely to the priorities of the school development plan. It should operate within the context of whole-school policies including the equal opportunities policy and the performance management policy.

Purpose
Its main purpose is improving the quality of teaching and learning through:
• identifying and disseminating good practice;
• monitoring the effectiveness of school policies in raising standards and complying with school and statutory requirements;
• identifying areas for future development.

Management responsibility
XX will have overall responsibility for managing the observation programme.

Code of conduct
Observers should ensure that they comply with the code of conduct attached as Appendix 1 to this document. Observers and teachers should be familiar with key whole-school policies, e.g. teaching and learning, curriculum, assessment, EAL, equal opportunities.

Monitoring
1 Department
Heads of department, in co-operation with other senior departmental staff, should observe each department member once in each academic year, at times to be arranged within the department. This should be part of normal routine requiring little or no cover requirement but, if necessary, standards funding may be applicable and release time negotiated. The departmental observation timetable should be given to the line manager, with a copy to the deputy headteacher if not the line manager.

2 Key stage/year group
Key stage leaders and year heads should undertake a systematic monitoring of tutor time and PSHE which will include observing each tutor group once in an academic year. Little or no cover should be required but, if necessary, standards funding may be applicable and release time negotiated. The focus should relate to priorities in the SDP.

3 Senior management team
Members of the senior management team are expected to monitor each of the departments for which they are responsible. The target is for each to observe XX lessons over the academic year, spread to provide general information and also specific information to support the current focus. The timing should be negotiated with each department. No cover requirement.

4 Governors
Governors should, as part of their support for subjects or a year group, undertake some observation when visiting the department. The observation must follow the guidance provided for governors. The programme should be by arrangement with the head of department or deputy head. The visit should result in a brief report to the governing body using the standard format.

Staff development (identifying and sharing good practice)
In addition to monitoring, it is good practice within a department for staff to have the opportunity to observe each other. The head of department should make the appropriate arrangements in consultation with subject staff. This will normally be part of the departmental development plan and a bid can be made for standards funding if any cover is essential. In relation to the year groups and key stages, the key stage leaders should make similar arrangements.

Induction of newly qualified teachers (NQTs)
The statutory requirements for the induction of NQTs include classroom observation. This is organised by each NQT's mentor in consultation with the school co-ordinator for induction.

Beginning teachers
The school is involved with XX higher education institutes in a programme of work for students in training. The observation requirements are agreed with the institutions, as are the criteria and the observation forms. The school professional tutor is responsible for this programme in consultation with heads of department.

Criteria for observation
All classroom observation should be undertaken in accordance with specific criteria. In some instance these will be national, for example, the induction standards for NQTs are published. In other cases the school's general policy on teaching should form the basis of the criteria for observation. This is attached as Appendix X to this policy.

Observation records
Observation forms may vary according to the purpose for which the observation is being undertaken. The school has a standard form for a general observation and also outlines which may be adapted for specific purposes. Whenever a lesson is observed, the observer should give a copy of the observation notes to the teacher concerned and agree a time for feedback and discussion of the lesson. The school guidance on lesson observation is attached as Appendix X to this policy.

Feedback
This should normally take place within 24 hours of the observation. It should be private and uninterrupted but need not take hours. About 10 to 15 minutes per observation should be sufficient. If more time than this is needed it suggests that there may be more serious issues which need to be resolved. It is good practice to give the teacher time to comment on his or her perceptions of the lesson and for the observer to start by identifying strengths and, where relevant, improvement since the last observation. The agreed targets/points for development should normally be no more than two or three. Any professional development or support needs should be noted and passed to the relevant person within the department or campus or to the professional development co-ordinator.

Documentation
The observer and the teacher will keep copies of observation forms and any written comments. Where the observer is not the head of department or director of campus, a copy of the information will be sent to him/her. Summary information will be fed into whole-school policies.

Disputes
If the teacher disagrees with the observation report or has concerns about the process, this will be dealt with as any other professional disagreement, that is, through discussion between the two staff in the first instance and then involving the line management structure as necessary. At any meeting concerning a dispute, the staff concerned have the right to be accompanied by a friend.

Evaluation/reporting to governors
The deputy head will be responsible for providing an annual report to the headteacher and the governors, on the effectiveness of the programme as a whole not on the performance of individuals.

APPENDIX X: DRAFT CODE OF CONDUCT FOR OBSERVATION

- Make sure you follow the school policy for observation and other school policies as relevant.

- Be sensitive to the fact that observation can be stressful for teachers, however well you know each other even though you think you are friendly and non-threatening. Very experienced teachers can often be more nervous than inexperienced teachers, particularly if they are not used to being observed.

- Be on time for the lesson and try not to interrupt it on arrival and departure. When leaving, if a few words of thanks are not possible, at least indicate your thanks. Do not try to debrief at the end of the lesson unless this is what you have arranged.

- Arrange a feedback time and place within 24 hours of the observation.

- Observation sessions should normally be a full lesson, but this can be varied to suit particular circumstances, e.g. you may be concentrating on the start or finish of lessons and therefore only wish to spend 10 to 15 minutes in the room at the appropriate time. This is acceptable but please agree this with the teacher concerned.

- You will need to take notes while you are observing. It is sensible not to rush to judgement. Lessons often develop in a different way from what you might expect. Your records should make it clear that you have followed the school's guidance on teaching and learning. When you make judgements, as you must, make them clear and give as much specific evidence as possible to support these judgements. For example, if you say that standards are consistent with national expectations, the observation form should make it clear what the pupils know, understand and can do in the context of that lesson. If you think questioning skills are particularly good, note down examples of actual questions used. This level of detail will help you when it comes to feeding back.

- Give the teacher a copy of the observation form and any report you write after the feedback session. Try to limit any suggestions for development to no more than three or four main points, and agree these with the teacher. Destroy unnecessary paperwork.

- Agree the purpose of the observation and stick to the ground rules. If you have agreed with the teacher that you are going to talk to pupils, do this as much as possible without disrupting their work.

- Do not interfere with the way the class is being taught and/or managed, unless there is a real health and safety issue or not to do so would seriously compromise your position. If in doubt, leave the lesson and seek advice. Remember, this is not your class.

- Never allow yourself to be drawn into a position where you appear to be colluding with pupils against the teacher.

10 The school commitment

Finding the time

Probably the most common complaint or problem in schools is lack of time. Teachers and headteachers complain, with considerable justification, that it is difficult enough to implement all the curricular demands without having to find time to observe. There is, however, an overriding responsibility shared by everyone with a management role and that is to ensure that the school is providing its pupils with the best possible education. This puts monitoring and evaluation high on the agenda.

The freedom and responsibility of schools to make their own managerial decisions has brought with it the need for high quality information so that precious resources can be accurately targeted. Systematic observation will provide much of the information on which evaluation and hence decisions can be based.

What happens to the information from observation is therefore important to the school as well as to the individual teacher. If you have a direct responsibility for the work of the teacher, as head of department or year head, constructive observation and support are part of your monitoring. The observation should tell you how well school and departmental policies are being implemented, and how teachers and pupils are reacting to any changes.

Monitoring by itself is not enough. You and the school need to give thought to making sure that the school as well as the teacher benefits from the observation programme. Evaluating the information you gain from systematic observation should lead directly to improvements in your own work in managing your responsibilities or your department or your year team. As a manager you should identify what has worked or is working effectively, as well as what needs revision or further development. The information might confirm, for example, that the use of the school homework policy is consistent but that departmental procedures for standardising assessment and moderating work need to be sharpened up. This should then lead to a revision of departmental planning.

Senior staff may gain ideas which would help their own teaching and that of others. This opportunity to spread good practice, whether at the level of sharing a worksheet or the approach to teaching a whole topic or section of work, is important and they must make sure that they do not ignore it.

Observers should also feed relevant information into whole-school development planning. A head of department might note that a particular whole-school policy needs some review. It could be that lack of access to facilities at suitable times is hindering the use of ICT or that the school assessment and marking policy is now out of date. A year head might become aware that tutors are not confident to deliver all aspects of the PSHE programme and incorporate this into training programmes or materials for guidance.

In the light of the value to the school of observation, the question then becomes not 'how can we find the time?' but rather 'can we afford not to do this?' Schools have resolved the time issues in a variety of ways. Some schools have used observation by the senior management team first to introduce the concept. They have then followed this with a regular programme of middle management observation. Many have started with a rolling programme of departmental review. In this, heads of department work out their own observation schedule so that over an agreed period, for example one particular term, all teachers in that department can be observed. Year heads work out a similar schedule for observation during tutor periods. They would be expected to provide a report for the senior management team and governors to ensure that any issues arising contribute to whole-school development. If using non-contact time for observation does not wholly work, then a limited amount of cover may need to be budgeted for, but care should be taken that the same classes are not having to be covered too often.

Another approach to departmental review is to release one or more members of the senior management team and the head of department from their own timetables for one or two days, not necessarily consecutively but within a short period of time, to observe across the school. They will also look at planning and samples of work. They will feed back to individual teachers and analyse the information to identify common issues which can contribute to the faculty development plan. Any relevant matters can also then be fed into school development planning. The programme can be profitably undertaken when the faculty is a priority for review and development in the school development plan. Careful analysis of how the standards fund can be used may meet the costs of release for this and other arrangements.

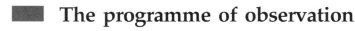 The programme of observation

Instituting and maintaining a programme of observation raise common issues in schools. These can affect the success of the programme and include:

- confidentiality;

- timing;

- additional workload;

- documentation;

- the validity of judgements.

The issues need to be resolved at a whole-school level, and for teachers to be convinced of the programme's fairness, there must be consistency across the school.

A school policy on observation which covers these will help to prevent many potential difficulties. The policy does not need to be long, but it should contain the following:

- a brief statement of principles: why observation is regarded as essential, what its main purposes are;

- responsibilities: who is responsible for what plus an outline (not a detailed) timetable of events;

- a succinct code of practice for observers: this should not try to cover every eventuality but give sensible guidance on issues such as behaviour, expectations and confidentiality. An example of such a code is given in Appendix 1 to the sample classroom observation policy in Chapter 9;

- reference to other relevant school policies with which observers and teachers should be familiar, e.g. school policies on teaching and learning, curriculum, assessment, EAL, equal opportunities;

- documentation: what will be retained and by whom, how relevant summary information will be fed into whole-school policies;

- a brief statement about how any disagreements will be resolved.

▆ Conclusion

Classroom observation, properly managed, is likely to be one of the most positive and constructive aspects of management and professional development. It gives senior and middle managers the opportunity to develop, encourage and praise their colleagues, and helps teachers to feel that they are recognised and valued. It enables all staff to learn from each other and to benefit from sharing expertise and ideas. Observation provides essential information about the reality of the day-to-day experience of pupils and the effectiveness of the school. It will help schools systematically to answer the questions – 'How far are we achieving what we set out to do?' and 'How can we do better?' Observation is about improving the education of pupils.

Appendix: Characteristics of effective teaching

(Key findings of Hay McBer's *Research into Teacher Effectiveness* – a report to the DfEE, June 2000)

Note: Appendices referred to here were part of the original full report and are included in the abbreviated website version on: www.dfee.gov.uk/teachingreforms

1.	*Key findings*
1.1	**Three factors**
	This chapter is a summary of the main outcomes from our work. It is intended to be of practical use to teachers and headteachers who are interested in what we found to be important in effective teaching.
1.1.1.	Our research confirms much that is already
Distinctive and complementary factors	known about the attributes of effective teaching. It also adds some new dimensions that demonstrate the extent to which effective teachers make a difference for their pupils. We found three main factors within teachers' control that significantly influence pupil progress:

- teaching skills;
- professional characteristics; and
- classroom climate.

Each provides distinctive and complementary ways that teachers can understand the contribution they make. None can be relied on alone to deliver value-added teaching.

The measures of teacher effectiveness

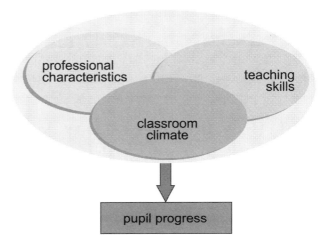

1.1.2	The three factors are different in nature. Two of
How the factors	them – professional characteristics and teaching
interact	skills – are factors which relate to what a teacher

The three factors are different in nature. Two of them – professional characteristics and teaching skills – are factors which relate to what a teacher brings to the job. The professional characteristics are the ongoing patterns of behaviour that combine to drive the things we typically do. Amongst those things are the 'micro-behaviours' covered by teaching skills. Whilst teaching skills can be learned, sustaining these behaviours over the course of a career will depend on the more deeply seated nature of professional characteristics. Classroom climate, on the other hand, is an output measure. It allows teachers to understand how the pupils in their class feel about nine dimensions of climate created by the teacher that influence their motivation to learn.

1.1.3
An example

So, for example, a teacher may have – amongst other things – the professional characteristic of **Holding People Accountable**, which is the drive and ability to set clear expectations and parameters and to hold others accountable for performance. Such a pattern of behaviour could make it more natural for this teacher to exhibit teaching skills like providing opportunities for students to take responsibility for their own learning, or correcting bad behaviour immediately. And the impact of these teaching skills, regularly exhibited, might be that pupils feel that there is a higher degree of **Order** in their class, or that there is the emotional **Support** needed to try new things.

1.1.4
Teachers are not clones

It should be noted, however, that this is only an example. In other circumstances, with different pupils, in a different context, other approaches might have been more effective. There is, in other words, a multiplicity of ways in which particular patterns of characteristics determine how a teacher chooses which approach to use from a repertoire of established techniques in order to influence how pupils feel.

1.1.5
A summary of how the model works

All competent teachers know their subjects. They know the appropriate teaching methods for their subjects and curriculum areas, and the ways pupils learn. More effective teachers make the most of their professional knowledge in two linked ways. One is the extent to which they deploy appropriate teaching skills consistently and effectively in the course of all their lessons – the sorts of teaching strategies and techniques that can be observed when they are at work in the classroom, and which underpin the national numeracy and literacy strategies. The other is the range and intensity of the professional characteristics they exhibit – ongoing patterns of behaviour which make them effective.

Pupil progress results from the successful application of subject knowledge and subject teaching methods, using a combination of appropriate teaching skills and professional characteristics. Professional characteristics can be assessed, and good teaching practice can be observed.

Classroom climate provides another tool for measuring the impact created by a combination of the teacher's skills, knowledge and professional characteristics. Climate is a measure of the collective perceptions of pupils regarding those dimensions of the classroom environment that have a direct impact on their capacity and motivation to learn.

Taken in combination, these three factors provide

valuable tools for a teacher to enhance the progress of their pupils.

1.1.6
Factors that do not contribute

On the other hand, we found that biometric data (i.e. information about a teachers' age and teaching experience, additional responsibilities, qualifications, career history and so on) did not allow us to predict their effectiveness as a teacher. Effective and outstanding teachers came from diverse backgrounds. Our data did not show that school context could be used to predict pupil progress. Effective and outstanding teachers teach in all kinds of schools and school contexts. This means that using biometric data to predict a teacher's effectiveness could well lead to the exclusion of some potentially outstanding teachers. This finding is also consistent with the notion that pupil progress outcomes are affected more by a teacher's skills and professional characteristics than by factors such as their sex, qualifications or experience.

1.1.7
Modelling the impact of the three factors

We used start-of-year and end-of-year pupil attainment data to underpin our assessment of relative effectiveness based on value added. Using this knowledge and the outcomes from our research described below, we have been able to model the impact teachers have on the classroom climate, how that climate affects pupil progress and what aspects of teaching skills and behavioural characteristics had most impact on climate.

1.1.8
Predicting over 30% of the variance in pupil progress

Our findings suggest that, taken together, teaching skills, professional characteristics and classroom climate will predict well over 30% of the variance in pupil progress. This is very important for teachers because it gives them a framework for assessing how they achieve their results and for identifying the priorities for improvement. (See Appendix IV for a detailed examination of the analysis leading to this conclusion.)

1.1.9
Teachers make the difference

So we show that teachers really do make a difference. Within their classrooms, effective teachers create learning environments which foster pupil progress by deploying their teaching skills as well as a wide range of professional characteristics. Outstanding teachers create an excellent classroom climate and achieve superior pupil progress largely by displaying more professional characteristics at higher levels of sophistication within a very structured learning environment.

1.2 **Teaching skills**

1.2.1 *Definition* Teaching skills are those 'micro-behaviours' that the effective teacher constantly exhibits when teaching a class. They include behaviours like:

- involving all pupils in the lesson;
- using differentiation appropriately to challenge all pupils in the class;
- using a variety of activities or learning methods;
- applying teaching methods appropriate to the national curriculum objectives;
- using a variety of questioning techniques to probe pupils' knowledge and understanding.

The 35 behaviours we looked for are based on research conducted by Professor David Reynolds and other colleagues. They are clustered under the seven OFSTED inspection headings for ease of use:

The teaching skills

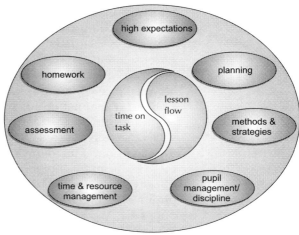

1.2.2 *Lesson flow and time on task* In addition to the micro-behaviours under the seven inspection headings, teaching skills can be observed in terms of the way the lesson is structured and flows, and the number of pupils who are on task through the course of the lesson.

1.2.3
Differentiating effective and outstanding

In primary schools, the outstanding teachers scored higher on average in four out of the seven clusters: **High Expectations**, **Time and Resource Management**, **Assessment**, and **Homework**. In secondary schools there was stronger differentiation covering all clusters, but it was particularly evident in **High Expectations**, **Planning**, and **Homework**.

1.2.4
Teaching skills described

Our lesson observations revealed that in classes run by effective teachers, pupils are clear about what they are doing and why they are doing it. They can see the links with their earlier learning and have some ideas about how it could be developed further. The pupils want to know more. They understand what is good about their work and how it can be improved. They feel secure in an interesting and challenging learning environment. And they support one another and know when and where to go for help. The research shows the criticality of the teacher in the pupil learning process. The effective teachers whom we observed and studied were very actively involved with their pupils at all times. Many of the activities were teacher-led. They created maximum opportunities to learn and no time was wasted. The environment was very purposeful and businesslike. But at the same time there was always a great deal of interaction between teacher and pupils.

One factor that led to this purposeful learning environment was the range of effective teaching skills and techniques deployed by the teacher in the classroom. The following paragraphs describe these skills and techniques in detail.

1.2.5
High expectations

Effective teachers set **High Expectations** for the pupils and communicate them directly to the pupils. They challenge and inspire pupils, expecting the most from them, so as to deepen their knowledge and understanding. The most effective teachers determine the appropriateness of objectives for pupils by some form of differentiation. At its lowest level, this means expecting different outcomes from pupils of varying ability. At a more sophisticated level, teachers know and use an extensive repertoire of means of differentiation – so that they are able to cope with the needs of more and less able pupils. But within these parameters effective teachers are relentless in their pursuit of a standard of excellence to be achieved by all pupils, and in holding fast to this ambition. These expectations are high, clear and consistent.

Key questions:
1. Does the teacher encourage high standards of
■   effort?
■   accuracy?
■   presentation?
2. Does the teacher use differentiation appropriately to challenge all pupils in the class?
3. Does the teacher vary motivational strategies for different individuals?
4. Does the teacher provide opportunities for students to take responsibility for their own learning?
5. Does the teacher draw on pupil experiences or ideas relevant to the lesson?

1.2.6
Planning

Effective teachers are good at **Planning**, setting a clear framework and objectives for each lesson. The effective teacher is very systematic in the preparation for, and execution of each lesson. The lesson planning is done in the context of the broader curriculum and longer-term plans. It is a very structured approach beginning with a review of previous lessons, and an overview of the objectives of the lesson linked to previous lessons and, where appropriate, the last homework assignment. Where homework is set (normally in secondary schools and for older primary pupils), the teacher often spends 5–10 minutes reviewing what pupils have learnt from it.

The effective teacher communicates the lesson content to be covered and the key activities for the duration of the lesson. Material is presented in small steps, with opportunities for pupils to practise after each step. Each activity is preceded by clear and detailed instructions. But the planning also takes into account the differing needs of pupils, including those with specific learning difficulties. For pupils, there is clarity of what they are doing, where they are going and how they will know when they have achieved the objectives of the lesson.

Effective teachers create the time to review lesson objectives and learning outcomes at the end of each lesson. Some teachers employ a **Tactical Lesson Planning** approach which describes both the content of lesson and the learning objectives, and the methods to be employed. But the focus of the planning activity is on pupil learning outcomes.

In some schools, particularly special schools, the highly effective teachers involve support staff in the preparation of the curriculum/lesson plans, and outline to them the role they are expected to play.

Key questions:

1. Does the teacher communicate a clear plan and objectives for the lesson at the start of the lesson?
2. Does the teacher have the necessary materials and resources ready for the class?
3. Does the teacher link lesson objectives to the National Curriculum?
4. Does the teacher review what pupils have learned at the end of the lesson?

1.2.7
Methods and strategies

Effective teachers employ a **Variety of Teaching Strategies** and techniques to engage pupils and to keep them on task. In our observations we saw effective teachers doing a great deal of active teaching. Many of the activities were led by the teacher. The teachers presented information to the pupils with a high degree of clarity and enthusiasm and, when giving basic instruction, the lessons proceeded at a brisk pace. Nevertheless, there was, in the majority of the classes, a range of teaching approaches and activities designed to keep the pupils fully engaged. Individual work and small group activities were regularly employed as ways of reinforcing pupil learning through practice and reflection.

However, it was evident that when the effective teachers were not actively leading the instructions they were always on the move, monitoring pupils' focus and understanding of materials. Content and presentation were varied to suit the needs of the class and the nature of learning objectives.

So what we saw effective teachers doing was a great deal of direct instruction to whole classes, interspersed with individual and small group work. But the active style of teaching does not result in passive pupils. Rather, there is a great deal of interaction between teacher and pupils. Effective teachers ask a lot of questions and involve the pupils in class discussion. In this way the pupils are actively engaged in the lesson, and the teacher is able to monitor pupils' understanding and challenge their thinking by skilful questioning. It is evident that effective teachers employ a sophisticated questioning approach – ranging from asking many brief questions on main and supplementary points, to multiple questioning of individuals to provide greater understanding and challenge.

Key questions:

1. Does the teacher involve all pupils in the lesson?
2. Does the teacher use a variety of activities/ learning methods?
3. Does the teacher apply teaching methods appropriate to the National Curriculum objectives?
4. Does the teacher use a variety of questioning techniques to probe pupils' knowledge and understanding?
5. Does the teacher encourage pupils to use a variety of problem-solving techniques?
6. Does the teacher give clear instructions and explanations?
7. Does practical activity have a clear purpose in improving pupils' understanding or achievement?
8. Does the teacher listen and respond to pupils?

1.2.8
*Pupil
management/
discipline*

Effective teachers have a clear strategy for **Pupil Management**. A sense of order prevails in the classroom. Pupils feel safe and secure. This pupil management strategy is a means to an end: allowing maximum time for pupils to be focused on task, and thus maximising the learning opportunity. Effective teachers establish and communicate clear boundaries for pupil behaviour. They exercise authority clearly and fairly from the outset, and in their styles of presentation and engagement they hold the pupils' attention. Inappropriate behaviour is 'nipped in the bud' with immediate direct action from the teacher. Some effective teachers employ a 'catch them being good' policy whereby pupil behaviour which is appropriate and on task is recognised and reinforced by praise. One outstanding teacher referred to the importance of the 'lighthouse effect' – being aware of everything going on in the classroom and having 360° vision. In those schools where there was a likelihood of a high incidence of pupil misbehaviour, the effective teachers employed a very structured behavioural approach to each lesson, e.g. standing at the door to greet pupils; commanding attention at the beginning of the lesson; taking action on latecomers; taking direct and immediate action on inappropriate behaviours. The most effective teachers had a longer-term strategy of getting to know the pupils with behavioural problems. In other words the highly effective teacher is able to create an environment in which all pupils can learn by employing direct means of pupil management to ensure that disruption to learning is minimised and pupils feel safe and secure.

Key questions:
1. Does the teacher keep the pupils on task throughout the lesson?
2. Does the teacher correct bad behaviour immediately?
3. Does the teacher praise good achievement and effort?

4. Does the teacher treat different children fairly?
5. Does the teacher manage non-pupils (support teachers/staff) well?

1.2.9
Time and resource management

Effective teachers **Manage Time and Resources** wisely. The effective management of pupils, time, resources and support promotes good behaviour and effective learning. Effective teachers achieve the management of the class by having a clear structure for each lesson, making full use of planned time, using a brisk pace and allocating their time fairly amongst pupils. The effective teachers start their lessons on time and finish crisply with a succinct review of learning. Where they are able to do so, pupils are encouraged to manage their own time well and to achieve what is required in the time available. The classrooms are effective learning environments in which activities run smoothly, transitions are brief, and little time is lost in getting organised or dealing with disruptions. In our observations we found that highly effective teachers managed to get well over 90% of the pupils focused on task over the course of a lesson.

In those schools where support and/or parental help was available, the effective teachers involved helpers in the lesson planning stage and in the execution of the lessons. In some instances, support staff were trained in aspects of pupil management, reading support and computer skills.

Key questions:
1. Does the teacher structure the lesson to use the available time well?
2. Does the lesson last for the planned time?
3. Are appropriate learning resources used to enhance pupils' opportunities?
4. Does the teacher use an appropriate pace?
5. Does the teacher allocate his/her time fairly amongst pupils?

1.2.10
Assessment

It is evident that effective teachers employ a range of **Assessment** methods and techniques to monitor pupils' understanding of lessons and work. These could be tests, competitions, questioning or regular marking of written work. The effective teachers look for gains in learning, gaps in knowledge and areas of misunderstanding through their day-to-day work with pupils. Also, effective teachers encourage pupils to judge the success of their own work and to set themselves targets for improvement. They also offer critical and supportive feedback to pupils.

Key questions:

1. Does the teacher focus on . . .
   - understanding and meaning?
   - factual memory?
   - skills mastery?
   - applications in real-life settings?
2. Does the teacher use tests, competitions, etc. to assess understanding?
3. Does the teacher recognise misconceptions and clear them up?
4. Is there evidence of pupils' written work having been marked or otherwise assessed?
5. Are pupils encouraged to do better next time?

1.2.11
Homework

An important part of the assessment process is the regular setting and marking of **Homework**, particularly in secondary schools. The effective teachers ensure that homework is integrated with class work, is tailored to individual needs and is regularly and constructively marked.

Key questions:

1. Is homework set either to consolidate or extend the coverage of the lesson?
2. Is homework which had been set previously followed up in the lesson?
3. Does the teacher explain what learning objectives pupils will gain from homework?

1.2.12
Time on task and lesson flow

Overall, effective teachers had well over 90% of the pupils on task through the lesson, and their lessons flowed naturally to achieve an appropriate balance between. . .

- whole class interactive;
- whole class lecture;
- individual work;
- collaborative group work;
- classroom management; and
- testing or assessment.

The full observation schedule used in our research appears at Appendix I. It has since been adapted by the DfEE as a standard observation tool which has been offered to all schools as part of the new performance management arrangements.

1.3 **Professional characteristics**

1.3.1 *Definition*
Professional characteristics are deep-seated patterns of behaviour which outstanding teachers display more often, in more circumstances and to a greater degree of intensity than effective colleagues. They are how the teacher does the job, and have to do with self-image and values; traits, or the way the teacher habitually approaches situations; and, at the deepest level, the motivation that drives performance.

1.3.2 *Five clusters*
From the in-depth interviews (behavioural event interviews) with the teachers in our sample we found that 16 characteristics contribute to effective teaching. Strength in five clusters is required. Certain different combinations of characteristics within these clusters can be equally effective. This is not a static 'one-size-fits-all' picture. Effective teachers show distinctive combinations of characteristics that create success for their pupils.

The model of professional characteristics

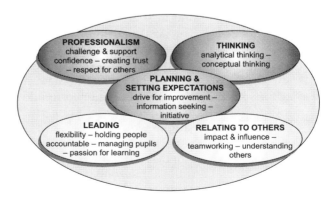

1.3.3
Characteristics flow from the data

The dictionary of characteristics (which may be found in section 2) and the descriptions of different levels for each characteristic were not part of a pre-existing model. They are defined by the data we collected from teachers.

1.3.4
What the dictionary contains

In the dictionary of professional characteristics, each characteristic is defined as succinctly as possible. It has a core question which helps teachers and their managers understand the essence of the characteristic. There is a short commentary on why it matters in the context of the teaching role. Examples of what it looks like at different levels of complexity or intensity are provided, along with a description of how the levels work so that they can be distinguished more easily. Finally, there is a list of the other characteristics with which it links most frequently in the research data.

1.3.5
Differentiating effective and outstanding . . .

The particular characteristics that emerge from our research represent what teachers actually do overtime, both in the classroom and outside it, to deliver results. We looked for a description of the combinations of characteristics (an 'algorithm') which would enable us to sort our sample with around 80% accuracy between outstanding and typical.

. . . in different roles and levels

And we looked for algorithms which would accurately describe effective performance at the threshold, at main professional grade, at AST, and in shared leadership positions.

The AST algorithm accurately sorts outstanding and typical performers 72% of the time in a small sample. The threshold algorithm accurately sorts 86% of the time. The main professional grade algorithm is designed to allow all effective teachers to pass, and over 80% of the total sample would do this. We did not see evidence of particular middle manager patterns in primary schools, but we were able to arrive at an algorithm for secondary heads of department which accurately sorted 78% of the time. The shape of this middle manager model was very similar to the shared leadership model developed in a parallel research project investigating the characteristics of deputy headteachers and newly-appointed heads.

It was not evident from our research that it would be possible or appropriate to differentiate between subjects, phases, or within professional levels (e.g. threshold).

1.3.6
How teachers display the professional characteristics

The professional characteristics fall into five clusters: **Professionalism, Thinking, Planning and Setting Expectations, Leading** and **Relating to Others**. Effective teachers need to have some strengths in each of them. On the following pages we describe the characteristics cluster by cluster.

1.3.7
Professionalism cluster

The driver for teachers is a core of strongly held and enacted values which, taken together, are a powerful basis for professionalism. There are four characteristics which describe this cluster or group of characteristics.

Respect for Others underpins everything the effective teacher does, and is expressed in a constant concern that everyone should treat pupils and all members of the school community with respect. Effective teachers explicitly value others, value the diversity in the school community, and retain their respect of others even when sorely tried. Outstanding teachers take a number of steps over time to create a feeling of community in the class or in the school. Effective teachers also provide **Challenge and Support** – a 'tough caring' where they not only cater for pupils' needs for physical and psychological safety but, crucially, repeatedly express positive expectations and build pupils' self-esteem and belief that they can succeed, as learners and in life. Threshold and outstanding teachers do everything in their power to ensure all pupils get the best deal possible from their education. Effective teachers show **Confidence** in most situations, expressing optimism about their own abilities and making an active contribution in meetings. Over time this confidence grows, so that a teacher sees him or herself as a fully rounded professional, able to succeed in most circumstances. Effective teachers take a full part in moving the school forward and improving its effectiveness, drawing on their experience to help shape policies and procedures.

They have emotional resilience in dealing with challenging pupils and situations where, because they have a range of professional skills and have already experienced similar challenges, they are able to keep calm. This ability is fuelled by a conviction about the importance and value of what they are doing as highly effective practitioners in shaping the future of their pupils. They identify with the job and see the challenge of an increasingly 'front line' role as part of the territory. The very best go even further, rising to stretching challenges and expressing a belief that they will succeed against the odds.

Effective teachers are consistent and fair, **Creating Trust** with their pupils because they honour their commitments. They are genuine, generate an atmosphere where pupils can express themselves and not be afraid of making mistakes – an important starting point for learning. They are a dependable point of reference in what, for many pupils, is a turbulent world. As they progress in the profession, increasingly they live up to their professional beliefs. These characteristics, taken together, result in an underlying concern for pupils and their achievement. Effective teachers are quite evidently there to support their pupils, and their sense of vocation is at the heart of the model of effective teaching.

Characteristic definitions:

Challenge and Support: A commitment to do everything possible for each pupil and enable all pupils to be successful.

Confidence: The belief in one's ability to be effective and to take on challenges.

Creating Trust: Being consistent and fair. Keeping one's word.

Respect for Others: The underlying belief that individuals matter and deserve respect.

1.3.8
*Thinking
cluster*

The **Thinking** that effective teachers bring to the job is characterised by **Analytical Thinking** – the drive to ask why, to see cause and effect and think ahead to implications; and **Conceptual Thinking** – the ability to see patterns in behaviour and situations and, at the level of outstanding teaching, to adapt creatively and apply concepts, ideas and best practice. Effective teachers plan individual lessons, units and programmes of work soundly based on data and evidence-led assessment of pupils, and evaluation of results. They attend to what is actually happening and have a logical, systematic approach to the job, looking after the details in order to achieve success for all pupils. Outstanding teachers are able to analyse many more variables in a complex situation, and have the ability to trace many possible causes and effects.
Characteristic definitions:
Analytical Thinking: The ability to think logically, break things down, and recognise cause and effect.
Conceptual Thinking: The ability to see patterns and links, even when there is a lot of detail.

1.3.9
*Planning and
setting
expectations
cluster*

By adopting a professional approach, teachers' energy can be channelled into **Planning and Setting Expectations**, targeting the key elements which will make the most difference to their pupils, and the results they are able to achieve. Teaching is a demanding role and the pace of change rapid.
Effective teachers are committed to meeting the needs of all pupils and to including everyone in the class. This means carefully prioritising and targeting their efforts so that all pupils get their fair share of attention and everyone achieves good results. There are three characteristics which group together in this cluster of the model. In terms of **Drive for Improvement,** all effective teachers want not only to do a good job but also to set and measure achievement against an internal standard of excellence. Threshold teachers seek to do everything they can to improve the

attainment of their pupils, to make the school itself more effective in raising achievement, and to reflect on and improve their own professional practice. Outstanding teachers continuously set and meet ambitious targets for themselves and their pupils. They refer regularly to visible, quantifiable and tangible measures; and they focus on whether they and the school really are making a difference and adding value to pupils.

Information Seeking works with this drive for results. All effective teachers ask questions to get a first-hand understanding of what is going on. At threshold level, teachers dig deeper to find out more about their pupils and their classes, so they can set differentiated programmes of work, and targets that start from an understanding of prior attainment and potential performance. Outstanding teachers continually gather information from wider and more varied sources and use their own systems progressively to do so.

All effective teachers use their **Initiative** to seize immediate opportunities and sort out problems before they escalate, and are able to act decisively in a crisis situation. Pupils in their classes will be aware of the 'lighthouse effect', the habitual scanning by which effective teachers appear to pick up everything that is going on.

Threshold and outstanding teachers show a much stronger ability to think and act ahead, to seize a future opportunity, or to anticipate and address future problems: for example, to enrich the curriculum or to bring additional resources into the school.

Characteristic definitions:

Drive for Improvement: Relentless energy for setting and meeting challenging targets, for pupils and the school.

Information Seeking: A drive to find out more and get to the heart of things; intellectual curiosity.

Initiative: The drive to act now, to anticipate and pre-empt events.

1.3.10
Leading cluster

In terms of delivery of effective teaching and learning, teachers take a role in **Leading** others. There are four characteristics in this cluster of the model.

In their drive to motivate and provide clear direction to pupils, all effective teachers are adept at **Managing Pupils**. They get pupils on task, clearly stating learning objectives at the beginning of a lesson and recapping at the end, and giving clear instructions about tasks. They keep pupils informed about how the lesson fits into the overall programme of work, and provide feedback to pupils about their progress. Threshold teachers are more consistently able to make every lesson effective and remove any barriers to the effective working of the class and groups within it. Outstanding teachers go further, going out of their way to get extra materials or extra resources they need. Many of them are able consistently to enthuse pupils in their classes and achieve full involvement, creating a positive, upbeat atmosphere to secure the results planned.

All teachers demonstrate a **Passion for Learning** by providing a stimulating classroom environment, giving demonstrations, checking understanding and providing whole class, group and individual practice in using and applying skills and knowledge. They consistently differentiate teaching and learning when it is appropriate to do so, to help all pupils learn and to tailor opportunities to practise, embed and extend new learning to each pupil. Outstanding teachers are able to go further in the extent to which they are consistently able to support all pupils in their classes to think for themselves, and to deepen their understanding of a subject or a skill.

Effective teachers show a high degree of **Flexibility.** Not only are they open to new approaches and able to adapt procedures to meet the demands of a situation, but they are also flexible in the classroom and outside. At threshold level, when they need to change direction they do so fluently. If they are not getting through to a pupil or a class they approach things from another angle, accessing a wide repertoire of teaching techniques and methods to do so. They are also able to deviate from and return to a lesson plan, to take advantage of an unexpected occurrence or to pursue something in which pupils show particular interest.

Because effective teachers are determined that pupils will achieve good results, they are committed to **Holding People Accountable** – both pupils and others with whom they work in the school. They set clear expectations of behaviour and for performance, and contract with pupils on these, setting clear boundaries for what is acceptable. In this way they provide a clear framework, routines and security in which work can take place. Teachers at threshold level go further, in that they constantly keep pupils and others up to the mark and get them to do what they had undertaken to do. Outstanding teachers consistently and successfully confront poor performance, taking timely and decisive action to ensure performance recovery.

Characteristic definitions:

Flexibility: The ability and willingness to adapt to the needs of a situation and change tactics.

Holding People Accountable: The drive and ability to set clear expectations and parameters and to hold others accountable for performance.

Managing Pupils: The drive and the ability to provide clear direction to pupils, and to enthuse and motivate them.

Passion for Learning: The drive and an ability to support pupils in their learning, and to help them become confident and independent learners.

1.3.11
Relating to others cluster

Underpinning their leadership role, effective teachers are good at **Relating to Others**. In this cluster there are three characteristics. Effective teachers have strengths in **Understanding Others**, working out the significance of the behaviour of pupils and others, even when this is not overtly expressed. Outstanding and threshold teachers have a deep insight into the reasons for the ongoing behaviour of others: why pupils and others act the way they do. They have an insight into what will motivate others, or what may be obstructing learning.

It also means they can use their ability to **Impact and Influence** pupils to perform. All effective teachers use several different logical arguments to persuade. At threshold level, teachers are able consistently to calculate what will appeal to pupils – and others – so that learning can be vivid, memorable and fun. Outstanding teachers go further in their use of indirect influence, with and through others, to bring about positive educational outcomes. This, together with their own deep understanding of and enthusiasm for their subject or specialism, works as a strong influencing factor on pupils and how they engage with learning.

Finally, all effective teachers are good at **Teamworking**. Not only do they provide help and support to colleagues, but they also seek and value their ideas and input. Outstanding teachers are active in building team spirit and the 'feel good' factor, so that people in the school feel part of the team, identify with it, and are proud of what it is doing to support pupils in achieving their full potential, as learners and in life.

Characteristic definitions:

Impact and Influence: The ability and the drive to produce positive outcomes by impressing and influencing others.

Teamworking: The ability to work with others to achieve shared goals.

Understanding Others: The drive and ability to understand others, and why they behave as they do.

(The full dictionary of professional characteristics appears in section 2 of Research Report 216).

1.4   **Classroom climate**

1.4.1

Definition   Classroom climate is defined as the collective perceptions by pupils of what it feels like to be a pupil in any particular teacher's classroom, where those perceptions influence every student's motivation to learn and perform to the best of his or her ability.

1.4.2
Creating effective learning environments

Our research shows that effective teachers use their knowledge, skills and behaviours to create effective learning environments in their classrooms.

They create environments which maximise opportunities to learn, in which pupils are well managed and motivated to learn. From the pupils' perspectives, they are mostly looking to the teacher to create a sense of security and order in the classroom, an opportunity to participate actively in the class and for it to be an interesting and exciting place.

1.4.3
Climate dimensions

Each climate dimension represents an aspect of how the pupils feel in that classroom. They are defined as follows:

1. **Clarity** about the purpose of each lesson. How each lesson relates to the broader subject, as well as clarity regarding the aims and objectives of the school.
2. **Order** within the classroom, where discipline, order and civilised behaviour are maintained.
3. A clear set of **Standards** as to how pupils should behave and what each pupil should do and try to achieve, with a clear focus on higher rather than minimum standards.
4. **Fairness:** the degree to which there is an absence of favouritism, and a consistent link between rewards in the classroom and actual performance.
5. **Participation:** the opportunity for pupils to participate actively in the class by discussion, questioning, giving out materials, and other similar activities.
6. **Support:** feeling emotionally supported in the classroom, so that pupils are willing to try new things and learn from mistakes.
7. **Safety:** the degree to which the classroom is a safe place, where pupils are not at risk from emotional or physical bullying, or other fear-arousing factors.

8. **Interest:** the feeling that the classroom is an interesting and exciting place to be, where pupils feel stimulated to learn.

9. **Environment:** the feeling that the classroom is a comfortable, well organised, clean and attractive physical environment.

1.4.4
Constructing primary and secondary questionnaires

The classroom climate pilot work we undertook with groups of teachers and pupils enabled us to test and refine a 27-question (three questions per dimension) Primary School Classroom Climate Questionnaire (PSCCQ), and a 57-question (6 to 7 questions per dimension) Secondary School Classroom Climate Questionnaire (SSCCQ). Both questionnaires assessed the nine climate dimensions of **Clarity, Order, Standards, Fairness, Participation, Support, Safety, Interest,** and **Environment**. The secondary questionnaire, unlike the primary, asked students to assess current and desired future classroom climate. Our main phase of classroom climate research, based on a broad sample of primary and secondary school classes, demonstrated the reliability of both climate questionnaires. Furthermore, the associations between the nine climate dimensions reveal somewhat similar latent structures in both the PSCCQ and the SSCCQ. An example of a question drawn from the order dimension, for both questionnaires, is shown below, and the questions from each relating to fairness appear at the end of Appendix IV.

PSCCQ:

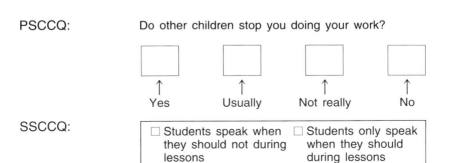

1.4.5
Latent variables

Our classroom climate analysis revealed three important underlying factors which are particularly significant to pupils' learning opportunity: **Lack of disruption**; **Encouragement to engage**; and **High expectations** (by the teacher). These 'latent variables' are important in helping teachers think about what they might do differently in order to have a bigger impact on pupil progress. Each variable has particularly strong links to two or more of the classroom climate dimensions as follows:

latent variable	linked climate dimensions **primary**	**secondary**
expectations	clarity standards	clarity standards
lack of disruption	order safety	order safety
encouragement to engage	support participation	participation fairness

These latent climate variables bear a resemblance to those described by Creemers and Reezigt (1999) in their work on classroom climate in the Netherlands. They identify four main climate factors: expectations on student outcomes (similar to **Expectations**); an orderly classroom environment (which captures some aspects of **Lack of Disruption**); well-functioning relationships in the classroom between teachers and students, and students and students (which captures some aspects of **Encouragement to Engage as well as Lack of Disruption**); and the physical environment of the classroom (similar to **Environment**, a climate dimension which tended to stand on its own, at least in our primary school classroom data).

1.4.5
Correlation with pupil progress

Our research also demonstrates a significant link between classroom climate and student academic progress. It seems likely, therefore, that both questionnaires measure aspects of classroom climate that are motivating and performance enhancing for students.

Pupil progress data for students from the primary classes in the classroom climate study correlated strongly with overall classroom climate ($r = .51$, $p < .01$), as well as with the individual climate dimensions **Order**, **Safety** and **Environment**. This suggests that a pleasant physical environment combined with a lack of disruption is particularly important for academic progress in primary schools.

In secondary classes in the classroom climate study, pupil progress correlated strongly with the size of the gap between existing and desired future classroom climate (point-biserial $r = .56$, $t=2.00$, $p < .05$), as well as with the individual climate dimensions **Clarity**, **Order**, **Fairness**, **Support**, **Safety** and **Interest**. This would seem to indicate more complex, though consistent, influences on academic progress in secondary schools compared to primary.

1.4.6
Implications for teachers' development

Because classroom climate, as measured here, also shows significant relationships with teacher skills and professional characteristics, these findings have significant implications for teachers who wish to develop their teaching capability. To the degree that teachers can develop skills and characteristics that impact climate, so they can hope to more effectively motivate and engage their students.

1.4.7
Teachers' ability to predict their students' assessments

However, we also found that both primary and secondary school teachers were able only partially to predict their students' assessments of the climates within their classrooms. Hence, it seems that the representative sample of teachers in this study do not understand the climate that exists within their classrooms as well as they could. This suggests that, by administering the PSCCQ or SSCCQ to a sample of their students, teachers could gain greater insight into the climate within their classrooms. This would enable teachers to focus their effective teaching skills and characteristics on those aspects of the climate that should be improved, and, where necessary, help them better understand what aspects of their current teaching practices need to be developed.

1.4.8
Rapid feedback mechanism

Furthermore, waiting to see whether or not a teacher is capable of motivating students to perform, by measuring students' accomplishments at the end of the year, is a cumbersome and unwieldy way for teachers to discover whether their efforts to improve their teaching practices are bearing fruit. The measurement of whether any of the desired changes in classroom climate are taking place offers a much more rapid feedback mechanism to teachers regarding the degree to which changes in their teaching skills and professional characteristics are having the desired effects.

1.4.9
Information about impact of current behaviour

Despite the demonstrated impact of classroom climate on student motivation and performance, it is rare for British teachers, or teachers in other countries, to receive structured feedback on the climates they help create in their classrooms. We strongly recommend that this should change. If teachers are to make best use of the developmental feedback offered to them by teaching experts, they must have available to them information about the impact their current behaviour is having on classroom climate and students' motivation to perform.

1.4.10
Further research

An important topic deserving further research is the nature of the mechanisms that give rise to higher or lower levels of each climate dimension. There are some hints in the results of this study based on correlations between specific teaching skills and professional characteristics and the different climate dimensions. However, teachers would no doubt find it helpful if we could provide them with a clear understanding of exactly which teacher behaviours have the most impact on each climate dimension, and how rapidly these dimensions can be expected to improve as a result of more effective teaching practices.

1.5	**Combining the three factors**
1.5.1	We looked at how teaching skills, professional
Aims	characteristics and classroom climate worked

together to deliver pupil progress. Our aims were threefold:

- to simplify complexity;
- to identify links that will be helpful to teachers and their managers in improving outcomes for their pupils;
- to produce a model of teacher effectiveness which can, in the longer term, provide a basis for career and professional development at all levels of teaching.

We analysed the correlations between the different data sources to provide a detailed picture of exactly how effective teachers enable pupil progress. Once again, pupil progress data was used as the dependent variable for sample selection and analysis.

1.5.2
Links between
teaching skills,
climate and
pupil progress

Where primary teachers were observed in class and completed classroom climate surveys, observed teaching skills correlated significantly with overall climate, and in particular with **Support**, **Standards** and **Interest**. When the correlation of overall climate with particular aspects of good teaching practice was explored, there were particularly high correlations with **High expectations** and **Time and Resource Management**.

The correlations were dramatically improved when, instead of just taking observations and climate in isolation as predictors of progress, the two measures were used in combination. The measure of classroom climate measure, when combined with the measure of observable teaching skills, approximately doubled the accuracy of the prediction.

In the secondary classes for which both classroom climate data and observations of teaching practice were available, the teachers of classes with higher pupil progress demonstrated better overall teaching skills. There were significant correlations of climate with **High Expectations**, **Time and Resource Management**, **Planning** and **Homework**.

Because of a smaller sample size, it was not possible to explore the significance of combining climate and observation data to predict pupil progression in secondary schools. However the findings do suggest that, as in primary schools, good teaching skills have the potential to improve classroom climate and hence influence pupil progression.

1.5.3
Links between professional characteristics, climate and pupil progress

We looked in detail at the primary classes for which we had both data on the professional characteristics of the teacher (as evidenced from their in-depth interview) and data on the classroom climate and pupil progress. Significant correlations were found between pupil progress and characteristics, and – as with teaching skills – the significance of this correlation was approximately doubled when climate was used in combination with characteristics data to predict pupil progress.

Interview assessments of secondary school teachers in the sample were also higher for those teachers with higher overall climate ratings, in line with the notion that teachers' professional characteristics have the potential to improve classroom climate.

1.5.4
Things that made no significant difference

We looked at the age, sex, qualifications, and personal history of the teacher, as well as the school context (percentage of ethnic minority pupils, percentage of pupils receiving free school meals, size of school, etc.). We were not able to predict classroom climate or the pupil progress outcomes using any of these variables.

1.5.5
Summary

The integrating analyses found that pupil progress is most significantly influenced by a teacher who displays both high levels of professional characteristics and good teaching skills which lead to the creation of a good classroom climate, which puts this work firmly in the area of 'research which counts'. It is based on clear evidence of pupil progress and it gives to the teaching profession a framework for professional development that will make a difference. Above all, it re-emphasises how important and influential the teacher is in raising standards in schools whatever the existing situation.

References

Office for Standards in Education (OFSTED)

Framework 2000 – Inspecting Schools, January 2000, OFSTED.
Handbook for Inspecting Secondary Schools, January 2000, Stationery
    Office.

Department for Education and Employment (DfEE)

Hay McBer, *Research into Teacher Effectiveness* (Research Report 216),
    June 2000, DfEE.
Performance Management in Schools, June 2000, DfEE.
    This comprises:
        Performance Management Framework
        Model Performance Management Policy
        Guidance Note
Threshold Assessment, April 2000, DfEE.
    This comprises:
        Standards
        Threshold Application
        Guidance for Headteachers

Teacher Training Agency (TTA)

The English National Standards Pack, 1998, TTA.
    This comprises:
        Qualified Teacher Status
        Induction Year
        Subject Leaders
        National Standards for Headteachers 98
        National Standards for SEN Specialists 1999
        Advanced Skills Teachers
Supporting Induction: Guidance for Schools (Revised), May 2000.

Index